We Believe

**We Believe:
How the Nicene Creed
Can Deepen Your Faith**

We Believe
978-1-7910-3560-0
978-1-7910-3561-7 *eBook*

We Believe: DVD
978-1-7910-3564-8

We Believe: Leader Guide
978-1-7910-3562-4
978-1-7910-3563-1 *eBook*

We Believe

How the Nicene Creed Can Deepen Your Faith

Michael Carpenter

Abingdon Press | Nashville

We Believe

How the Nicene Creed Can Deepen Your Faith

Copyright © 2025 Abingdon Press
All rights reserved.

No part of this work may be reproduced or transmitted in any form or by any means, electronic or mechanical, including photocopying and recording, or by any information storage or retrieval system, except as may be expressly permitted by the 1976 Copyright Act, the 1998 Digital Millennium Copyright Act, or in writing from the publisher. Requests for permission can be addressed to Rights and Permissions, Abingdon Press, 810 12th Avenue South, Nashville, TN 37203-4704 or emailed to permissions@abingdonpress.com.

Library of Congress Control Number: 2025931069
978-1-7910-3560-0

Scripture quotations unless noted otherwise are taken from the New Revised Standard Version, Updated Edition. Copyright © 2021 National Council of Churches of Christ in the United States of America. Used by permission. All rights reserved worldwide.

Scripture quotations marked (KJV) are from The Authorized (King James) Version. Rights in the Authorized Version in the United Kingdom are vested in the Crown. Reproduced by permission of the Crown's patentee, Cambridge University Press.

MANUFACTURED IN THE UNITED STATES OF AMERICA

*To Alan, Laura, Robert, Adam, Kyle,
and every other link in faith's strong chain
who connect me to our living faith*

*To Rachel and our five phenomenal children,
for your constant and affirming support*

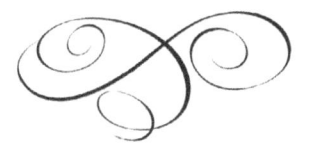

CONTENTS

Introduction ix

Chapter 1: We Believe in One God 1

Chapter 2: Of One Being with the Father 21

Chapter 3: For Us and for Our Salvation 41

Chapter 4: In Accordance with the Scriptures 59

Chapter 5: With the Father and the Son 77

Chapter 6: One, Holy, Catholic, and Apostolic 95

Conclusion: The Necessity of Nicaea Today 111

Notes 121

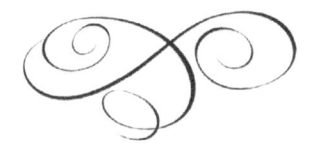

INTRODUCTION

Finding Bedrock

When I graduated high school, I left my small hometown in southern Oklahoma and moved to the state university for college. On a lark, I joined a fraternity, one founded on Christian principles, and moved into the fraternity house. There, I was exposed to a new range of religious identities I had never encountered before as a sixth-generation Methodist. One of my roommates was also Methodist, which was a comfort. But another roommate was Roman Catholic. There were Southern Baptists, Episcopalians, non-denominational Christians, and others as well.

We were a religiously active bunch. In addition to my becoming a United Methodist pastor, several of my fraternity brothers entered ministry. One is a priest in the Anglican Church of North America (ACNA) serving a church in California. Another is planting a Southern Baptist church in Texas. A third serves with his wife and children as Southern Baptist missionaries in Japan. A fourth was on the verge of becoming a Catholic priest before he met the girl of his dreams, closing the door on the life of an unmarried priest. Many others are committed laypeople in their local churches.

Introduction

You can imagine the conversations that we had about religion and faith. Plenty of our conversations turned heated as we debated why our denomination was right and everyone else was horribly misguided. I contend that I never lost one of those debates! (Though my fraternity brothers probably thought the same.) When we were in good moods, though, our conversations were positive. We were trying to discover where our understandings of faith lined up. Past all the things that separated us, we were digging down to the common core of our faith.

We disagreed about who could be baptized and how many times, but we agreed that it was an act of grace and new birth to be sought by all Christians. We disagreed about what happens in Holy Communion, but we agreed that it was an instrument for grace. We disagreed about which books belong in the Bible, but we agreed that whichever books were in there, they were the Word of God. And of course, we all agreed that God is one God in three Persons, Father, Son, and Holy Spirit.

My friends and I eventually found a succinct summary of our shared faith. We discovered (or discovered for ourselves) the Nicene Creed. Everything we all agreed on was in there, and no one disagreed with any of its lines. The Nicene Creed became, and continues to be, a shared bedrock of our common faith. It has been a tool that has guided our discussions, a comfort in times of doubt and insecurity, and a compass pointing to the living God who inspired it.

This book unpacks and explains the Nicene Creed, the foundational statement of Christian belief that is now seventeen hundred years old. It is intended for any Christian, no matter your familiarity with the Nicene Creed. Maybe you recite the Nicene Creed, or the similar Apostles' Creed, in worship every week. My church does that, and it has been critical in growing and deepening our faith (more on that later).

Maybe this is the first time you've heard of the word *Nicene*. If that's you, you're not alone. Plenty of Christians have lived lives of

Introduction

great faith with little awareness of this foundational document. It is my hope, then, that this book will be a little like my process of discovery with my fraternity brothers. By diving into the words and story of the Nicene Creed, you will be strengthened in what you have already believed. And more than that, you will rediscover the bedrock of your faith, allowing you to build reliably upon it. Simply put, the Nicene Creed has the power to reawaken your faith and reinvigorate your life as a Christian.

> **The Nicene Creed has the power to reawaken your faith and reinvigorate your life as a Christian.**

What Is the Nicene Creed?

Before we get into the text of the Nicene Creed, we need to get on the same page. The Nicene Creed is the creed, or statement of faith, that was agreed upon at the Council of Nicaea (pronounced *ny-SEE-a*). Nicaea, as we'll see below, is the name of a city in modern-day Turkey where a churchwide council was held in AD 325. The council that was held there was the first of its kind.

For Christianity's first three hundred years, it faced persistent and sometimes violent repression. At various points, Christians were persecuted to different degrees, ranging from ostracism from their communities to torture and even death. And yet, by the grace of God and the power of the Holy Spirit, the Church grew. The Church grew as an underground (sometimes literally!) community of believers.

That all changed in the early 300s, when a new Roman emperor named Constantine rose to power. His affinity for Christianity brought the Church out of the shadows. For the first time, Christians could openly discuss their faith. This new level of exposure, however, also revealed problems. Different churches had developed different beliefs. As we'll see, some of these beliefs were incompatible with one another. So Emperor Constantine, not wanting his new religion to be filled with dissension and conflict, called for a gathering of leaders across the Church to meet at Nicaea in 325 to hammer out these differences.

One Spring in Nicaea

Nicaea, situated in modern-day Iznik, Turkey, was a beautiful town in the perfect spot. It was close to the metropolis of Constantinople, less than one hundred miles away. But it was also tucked out of the way, situated on the coast of a large and peaceful lake. For both practical and political reasons, it was the perfect spot to host this first churchwide, or ecumenical, council.

The council began in May AD 325. In attendance were 318 bishops from across the Roman Empire and even beyond it.[1] Each bishop brought with him an entourage of secretaries and staff, so that the total list of attendees likely topped 2,000. Most shocking, however, was the presence of Emperor Constantine himself at the council. It had been less than thirty years since a terrible persecution of Christians by a previous emperor, but now the emperor himself was sitting in support of the Church!

In addition to the Nicene Creed, the Council of Nicaea also deliberated on other matters. They settled the debate on when Easter was to be celebrated, as some churches had been celebrating it on days other than Sundays depending on the calendar. And like any good church meeting, there were issues of church governance to discuss, including the appointment of bishops and matters of discipline for clergy. The bulk of the council, however, was dedicated to debating the issues of doctrine, or beliefs, that were causing controversy. Those debates worked themselves out into what became the Nicene Creed.

Introduction

As we'll see in future chapters, the debates centered on how Jesus relates to God the Father.

A Roadmap to Nicaea

At this point, with talk about church meetings and Roman history, you may be thinking, "How could a stale and boring statement like the Nicene Creed transform my faith? Why do I need some ancient group of bishops to tell me how to experience God?" You wouldn't be alone in thinking that. These are similar questions to those that were once asked of author C. S. Lewis by a British Royal Air Force officer. That officer, recalling his time fighting in North Africa during World War II, said that he had experienced God in the desert there. And so, in the face of that experience, he asked Lewis what good was something like the Nicene Creed?

Lewis responded, "Now in a sense I quite agreed with that man. I think he had probably had a real experience of God in the desert. And when he turned from that experience to the Christian creeds, I think he really was turning from something real to something less real." Your experience of creeds like the Nicene Creed might be the same, especially if you're used to reciting them in a monotone droll during worship. If you agree with that British officer, listen to how Lewis continued:

> In the same way, if a man has once looked at the Atlantic from the beach, and then goes and looks at a map of the Atlantic, he also will be turning from something real to something less real: turning from real waves to a bit of coloured paper. But here comes the point. The map is admittedly only coloured paper, but there are two things you have to remember about it. In the first place, it is based on what hundreds and thousands of people have found out by sailing the real Atlantic. In that way it has behind it masses of experience just as real as the one you

Introduction

could have from the beach; only, while yours would be a single glimpse, the map fits all those different experiences together. In the second place, if you want to go anywhere, the map is absolutely necessary. As long as you are content with walks on the beach, your own glimpses are far more fun than looking at a map. But the map is going to be more use than walks on the beach if you want to get to America.[2]

I want you to think of the Nicene Creed as a map, one leading you to a fuller experience of God. It is a map drawn up by the experience of holy people under the inspiration of the Holy Spirit. You may, like that British officer, have already experienced God at some point in your life. If you have, great! Even for you, the Nicene Creed can lead you to places you haven't explored and experiences of God that lie still ahead.

> **I want you to think of the Nicene Creed as a map, one leading you to a fuller experience of God.**

And if you, like many, have never encountered God in a real, incredible, life-changing way, then the Nicene Creed is your faithful map. Your experience of God has been only on the edges, like seeing the ocean simply by walking along a beach. But if you are ready to make the journey from the shore to a transforming encounter with God, then get ready for the Nicene Creed to bring you into deeper waters. What is uncharted for you has been faithfully charted by the saints who met in Nicaea seventeen hundred years ago.

The Nicene Creed is a map, rich in detail and expansive in scope, like those foldable state maps my family used to bring on summer road trips before the advent of MapQuest and Google Maps. This book, then, is like those helpful charts and insets printed next to those maps, highlighting points of interest and guiding you in how to use

Introduction

the map. In this book, you'll be shown how to get the most out of the Nicene Creed as a map for a richer understanding of God. Here is a brief look at where this book will take you:

Chapter 1 begins with the creed's treatment of God the Father. It will introduce the concept of a creed as well as the scope of the council's task in drafting a creed. It also includes a discussion of how the Nicene Creed's insistence on one Almighty God is relevant to our faith today. Chapter 2 moves into the creed's language about Jesus Christ and his relationship to the Father. The central controversies debated at the Council of Nicaea are tackled in this chapter.

Chapter 3 covers the biographical details of Jesus's life included in the creed. Specifically, it details how Jesus's birth, life, and death were done, as the creed says, "for us and for our salvation." Chapter 4 finishes the material in the creed about Jesus, covering his resurrection, ascension, and second coming. The focus of this chapter is how this happened, in the words of the creed, "in accordance with the Scriptures."

Chapter 5 turns to the Holy Spirit. Here we will quickly see a controversy that still persists between some branches of Christianity before turning to a discussion of how the Holy Spirit continues to bring the Nicene Creed to life for us. Finally, chapter 6 deals with the conclusion of the creed and its treatment of the Church. It ends by tying the creed's hopeful description of the Church back to our use of the creed itself.

A Note on Language

Before we begin, there are a couple of conventions and shorthands to describe that will make the book clearer. The first is the name of the Nicene Creed itself. The version of the creed that Christians around the world recite regularly is not exactly the version approved at

Introduction

the Council of Nicaea. Rather, it is the version of the creed expanded at the Council of Constantinople in AD 381. Thus, the proper name for the creed is the Niceno-Constantinopolitan Creed. But, for the sake of brevity and clarity, this book follows the vast majority of the Church in referring to it simply as the Nicene Creed.

On the text of the Nicene Creed, there are several translations available. Just as there are many English translations of the Bible, which was written originally in Hebrew and Greek, there are different ways to translate the Nicene Creed. Generally, when this book quotes the Nicene Creed, it does so with the translation used by my United Methodist denomination, found in *The United Methodist Hymnal*. The full text of this translation is included at the end of this introduction. Instances where that translation falls short or varies significantly from other translations will be noted.

One topic that has gained attention in recent years is that of gendered and inclusive language. My chosen translation takes care of some of the issues that might arise here. For instance, it translates the creed as saying that Jesus "became truly human" instead of "became man," as some translations say. Beyond that, this study, along with my translation of the creed, retains the language of the first two Persons of the Trinity as "Father" and "Son." While God is clearly above gender and no words could ever capture the full divinity of the Godhead, this is the historic language of the creed and of Church tradition and is retained for that reason.

Finally, you will notice that the word *church* is sometimes capitalized as *Church* in this book. This book uses the capital *C* Church to denote the worldwide body of Christ that includes all Christians. The lowercase *c* church is used to denote individual congregations or denominations of Christians. That is, several churches exist within the global Church.

THE NICENE CREED

We believe in one God,
the Father, the Almighty,
maker of heaven and earth,
of all that is, seen and unseen.

We believe in one Lord, Jesus Christ,
the only Son of God,
eternally begotten of the Father,
God from God, Light from Light,
true God from true God,
begotten, not made,
of one Being with the Father;
through him all things were made.

For us and for our salvation
he came down from heaven,
was incarnate of the Holy Spirit and the Virgin Mary
and became truly human.
For our sake he was crucified under Pontius Pilate;
he suffered death and was buried.

On the third day he rose again
in accordance with the Scriptures;
he ascended into heaven
and is seated at the right hand of the Father.
He will come again in glory
to judge the living and the dead,
and his kingdom will have no end.

We believe in the Holy Spirit, the Lord, the giver of life,
who proceeds from the Father and the Son,
who with the Father and the Son
is worshiped and glorified,
who has spoken through the prophets.

We believe in one holy catholic and apostolic church.
We acknowledge one baptism
for the forgiveness of sins.
We look for the resurrection of the dead,
and the life of the world to come. Amen.

CHAPTER 1
We Believe in One God

We believe in one God,
the Father, the Almighty,
maker of heaven and earth,
of all that is, seen and unseen

Where to Begin?

If we wanted to boil down our faith to a single, succinct summary, how would we do it? The Bible, after all, has sixty-six books, which contain 1,189 chapters and (depending on your translation) over 750,000 words. People spend years in schools studying their faith, and there seems to be no end of Bible studies helping explain everything you could ever want to know about what Christians believe. (And it is not lost on me that the present book is yet another addition to this unending stream of studies!) To attempt to distill Christianity into, say, a single paragraph seems laughably absurd. But as we'll see, that is exactly what the Nicene Creed does.

We Believe

A creed is a formal statement of beliefs, and the Nicene Creed is the bedrock statement of what all Christians around the world believe. In a way, the Nicene Creed is a little like the "elevator pitch" that some people use to make sales or land a job. I was taught to make an elevator pitch back in my former life as a civil engineer. The concept is simple: Imagine that you are in an elevator with a potential employer or client. You have sixty seconds in that elevator ride to make the case for hiring you.

> **A creed is a formal statement of beliefs, and the Nicene Creed is the bedrock statement of what all Christians around the world believe.**

Luckily, as a United Methodist pastor who gets appointed to a church by my bishop, I haven't had to think about an elevator pitch in over a decade (thanks, Bishop!). But if I were to come up with one again, it would go something like this:

> My name is Michael Carpenter, and I am an ordained pastor in The United Methodist Church. I used to be a civil engineer, but then I followed a calling from God into ministry. God called me to ministry despite a lifelong stutter, proving that God has a sense of humor in who God calls to preach. But by God's grace, the Spirit's power, and good speech therapy, preaching and teaching are now some of my favorite things to do.
>
> I've served as a pastor for over a decade in churches of all shapes and sizes. I've been on a multi-pastor team at a church that worshiped fifteen hundred every week, and I've served a rural church as the sole pastor and only full-time staff. I am a sixth-generation Methodist, and I even met my wife at a Methodist college ministry. We now have five wonderful children that include two sets of twins. They think their dad's job is "talking to people" and "meetings," and most days they're not wrong.

We Believe in One God

What gets me out of bed each morning (besides the five kids I just mentioned) is the purpose I've found in walking with people in their faith journeys and the joy I feel when seeds of faith produce fruit in them and their community.

Elevator pitches are, by nature, brief. They can't mention everything but instead hit all the critical high notes. My elevator pitch didn't have time to mention my love of the Chicago Cubs baseball team, my candle-making hobby, or the time my rural church abolished over $3.5 million in medical debt in five states. In summaries like this, cuts have to be made, complex facts distilled, and themes summarized.

This is precisely what was done for the Christian faith in the Nicene Creed. In the year AD 325, a worldwide gathering of church leaders at the Council of Nicaea crafted an "elevator pitch" of sorts for our faith. By the time the council gathered, there were several other creeds and statements of faith scattered across the Church. The idea of synthesizing beliefs into a digestible, easy-to-memorize and recite format had taken hold in the earliest generation of the Church. Many believe that Paul was attempting to create the earliest surviving creed in 1 Timothy 3:16, which says,

> *He was revealed in flesh,*
> *vindicated in spirit,*
> *seen by angels,*
> *proclaimed among gentiles,*
> *believed in throughout the world,*
> *taken up in glory.*[1]

Over time, these creeds began to take a certain shape. They were organized in a "trinitarian" format, that is, broken out into sections about each Person of the Trinity: Father, Son, and Holy Spirit. This chapter traces the first section of the Nicene Creed and what it says about God the Father. As with the other sections of the creed, what

3

the Council of Nicaea has to say about God the Father has the power to draw us more deeply into our faith and our experience of God. Like an elevator pitch for God and the Church, the few, brief sentences invite us to get to know God better.

We start with the Nicene Creed's essential declaration about who God is, what God has done, and what God is like.

One God

Every participant of the Council of Nicaea was a follower of Jesus and thus looked to the Scriptures of Israel as true and authoritative. Many Christians today call this the "Old Testament," but in the days before the "New" Testament was compiled and adopted, it was simply "the Scriptures."

When the risen Jesus was walking with a pair of disciples on the road to Emmaus on Easter Sunday, Luke tells us that Jesus "interpreted to them the things about himself in all the scriptures" (Luke 24:27). When the apostle Paul wrote to encourage his protégé Timothy to hold to the true teachings of God, he wrote, "All scripture is inspired by God and is useful for teaching, for reproof, for correction, and for training in righteousness" (2 Timothy 3:16). In those New Testament verses and others, "Scripture" means the Old Testament.

Early in those Scriptures of Israel is an essential declaration about God's nature. It is found in Deuteronomy 6:4, "Hear, O Israel: the LORD our God, the LORD is one." In the Jewish community, these are the opening words of a prayer known as the *Shema* (*shema* being the Hebrew word for "hear," the first word of the declaration). This declaration guided the Council of Nicaea on how they were to begin their creed. "We believe in one God" connected their work to one of the earliest, most foundational tenets of their faith.

And while confessing belief in "one God" may not sound controversial to us today, it was scandalous and offensive to the Church's neighbors in its first three hundred years.

Roman Atheists

In those first three centuries, when traditional Romans considered their Christian neighbors, a word they used often to describe them was *atheist*. That is, they did not believe in the gods of Rome. Like many ancient kingdoms and empires, there was no shortage of gods to worship in ancient Rome. Every time a new territory was brought into the empire, that territory's gods were brought in as well. This is illustrated to humorous effect in Acts 17, when the apostle Paul arrives in Athens and sees among all their many shrines and temples one altar in particular with the inscription "To an unknown god." The Athenians were covering their bases, worshiping a god they hadn't heard of but were sure must exist!

In the Roman world, you could worship any god you liked, so long as you acknowledged that the Roman gods were in the mix, too. Imagine it like being a baseball fan. A Chicago Cubs fan moves from Illinois to Atlanta. She still proudly wears her Cubs jerseys, but maybe after a while buys an Atlanta Braves hat to fit in better with her new neighbors. Even if she remains a diehard Cubs fan her whole life, she isn't discounting the Braves' existence or rejecting her neighbors' love of them. Being a Christian in the Roman world, however, was like saying that there is only one team and that any other teams are pure fiction.

This was what put the early Christians at such odds with their pagan Roman neighbors. For the Nicene Creed to begin with the bold claim that "we believe in one God" was to say that all those other gods, known and unknown, were as dead as the stone their temples were carved from.

That thought is nothing new to those who worship the God of the Bible. Psalm 135 puts it bluntly:

> *The idols of the nations are silver and gold,*
>   *the work of human hands.*
> *They have mouths, but they do not speak;*
>   *they have eyes, but they do not see;*
>
> . . . .
>
> *Those who make them*
>   *and all who trust them,*
>   *shall become like them.*
>   *(Psalm 135:15-16, 18)*

With the clarity that Christians worship and believe in the one and only God, the council could then move on to describe who that one God is.

Our Father

The next thing the Nicene Creed says about God gets to the very heart of who God is. God is, the creed tells us, "the Father." This should be familiar to us, as Jesus begins the most famous prayer in Christianity with, "Our Father in heaven" (Matthew 6:9; you may remember it with a "who art" thrown in there). God being described as a father is a common feature of Scripture (see Isaiah 64:8; 1 Corinthians 8:6; and Galatians 4:6, among others), and it is a depiction that gets to the heart of how relational God is to us. There is something about God being our Father that reveals to us God's character and helps us relate to God better.

To see that, we can use an example from earthly parents. I am the father to five wonderful, and wonderfully different, children. As I write this, my oldest child is in elementary school, and my youngest children are twin infants. Sandwiched between them is another set of twins who are in preschool. I am a father to each of them, but I am not a father in the same way to each of them. My infants need to be fed, changed, and rocked to sleep. For the sake of my back, thanks be to God that my fifty-pound oldest child no longer needs to be rocked to sleep!

And on the other end of the spectrum, I expect more from my oldest. This is not only in terms of responsibilities but also relationship. I don't have to hold his hand, literally and figuratively, as much as I do for his preschool-aged sisters. But he and I are capable of having deeper conversations and more meaningful adventures together because of that increased maturity. Even my relationship with each of my four twins is different! Despite being the same age as and in constant proximity with their twins, they are unique. And because of that uniqueness, my fatherhood is unique to each of them.

> **As we grow spiritually, God our Father meets our needs, increasing the depth of our calling and equipping us in turn.**

God's fatherhood is similarly unique to each of us. When we first come to faith, we are spiritual infants (Hebrews 5:12), in need of more guidance and support. As we progress in discipleship, however, we move up to solid food. Maybe we even pick up a few chores in God's kingdom! And as we grow spiritually, God our Father meets our needs, increasing the depth of our calling and equipping us in turn.

Where does this end? When do we outgrow the need for our Father? We don't! Even now, as a man in his thirties and a father of five, I still need and desire a relationship with my earthly parents. True, I no longer need them to explain to me how taxes work or how to shop for cars. Instead, our conversations are deeper, fuller, with much communicated even in knowing silence. The relationship is different, but the love is the same. As a Methodist, I believe that we can grow spiritually to the point where we have been made perfect in God's love. Even at this stage of holiness, we will still need and desire our Father. The relationship will be different, but the grace will be the same.

As I said in the introduction to this book, the Nicene Creed is a map that can guide us to a deeper relationship with God. Here we see an opportunity to deepen that relationship, by examining where we are in our faith journey and where God is meeting us at that stage in the relationship.

Some people are brand-new to the faith and are spiritual infants. For them, God is holding them as closely as my wife cradles our newborns, lovingly providing for their every need. Others have grown into spiritual children. In this stage of "childlike faith," they are like most children: full of questions and full of wonder. At that stage, God is taking them by the hand and showing them the ropes of faith. At some point, people may mature into the "teenage" years of their faith. In this spiritual adolescence, they find themselves with crises of identity and with easy answers no longer cutting it. Even then, God is the loving Father still, giving space as needed but always being available all the same. Finally, some grow into spiritual adulthood, ready to live confidently into the calling that God has given them. These mature Christians don't need the safety of the nest; they need room to soar! Wherever we find ourselves along this spectrum, God is our Father, loving us and proud of us. I'll say it again: God is proud of you; God thinks the world of you. Really!

While referring to God as Father strikes an important note on God's familial and relational qualities, it didn't fully capture everything the Nicene participants wanted to say. So they turned to another scriptural title for God that communicates God's power and authority as well.

The Almighty

Back in seminary, my Church history class took a field trip to an Eastern Orthodox church in our town. If you think that as postgraduate students we had outgrown field trips, think again! It was a fascinating experience, not least because we got to meet the church's priest, who had formerly been a Southern Baptist preacher (more on him in chapter 6). The most incredible part of the excursion, though, was looking down over me from above.

If you visit an Eastern Orthodox sanctuary and look up, you'll be stopped by a breathtaking sight. Painted in the central dome above the sanctuary is usually a rendering of Jesus known as "Christ the Almighty."[2] If you have never seen one, make a plan to visit an Orthodox church sometime. There, surveying the Church with a gaze that exudes serene power, is a vision of God that exemplifies the title next included in the Nicene Creed.

While the painting in Orthodox churches depicts Jesus Christ as "the Almighty," in the Nicene Creed that title is given to God the Father. As we shall see, the creed has a number of instances in which titles and attributes are shared between Father and Son due to the relationship between them, so there is thus good reason to think "Almighty" would apply to both here as well. The title "the Almighty" traces, once again, to the Old Testament, in the form of the Hebrew term *El Shaddai*, usually translated "God Almighty." This is the name God reveals to Abram in Genesis 17 when God promises with him to make a great nation. Being *El Shaddai*, God Almighty, means that God has the power and authority to cause a ninety-nine-year-old man to become a father and a ninety-year-old woman to become a mother.

In the New Testament, the title *Almighty* is used ten times, once by Paul quoting the Old Testament and nine times in Revelation. In Revelation, the title is used to describe God's authority over all the events unfolding in the book's vivid narrative. In one of those verses, made famous by the "Hallelujah Chorus" of Handel's *Messiah*, the heavenly multitude cries, "Hallelujah! For the Lord God omnipotent reigneth" (Revelation 19:6 KJV).

The word *omnipotent* in the "Hallelujah Chorus" is translated in most modern translations as "Almighty," coming from the same Greek word.

When God's titles of "Father" and "the Almighty" are combined, the Nicene Creed begins to get the full range of God's majesty. God is at once our Father, a relational term that brings with it love and closeness, and the Almighty, a forceful term that has implications of power and authority. These are two sides of the same coin that is God, the First Person of the Trinity.

> **God is far above but never far off.**

In theology, there are terms for this polarity: the immanence and transcendence of God. God is *immanent*, that is, close enough to be known and approached. This is communicated in the familiar term "Father" in the creed. But at the same time, God is also transcendent, or outside of our perception or understanding. This is the sense we get from God being "the Almighty." The great tension of the Nicene faith is to hold tightly to both God's immanence and transcendence. God is far above but never far off.

Before moving on with what the Nicene Creed says our Almighty Father has done, let's linger a moment longer in the town of Nicaea to see what this means for us.

How Big Your God Is

The town of Nicaea, in addition to being the site of this important Church council, was the perfect getaway destination. It was close to the new capital of the Roman Empire but a little off the beaten path. To make the scene even more picturesque, it also sat comfortably on the eastern shore of the pristine and peaceful Lake Nicaea. This was a place where the Church's leaders and all their staff could withdraw from the clamor of the world, deliberate on matters of faith, and discern God's will in peaceful serenity.

I've never been to Nicaea, but I've been somewhere similar. My personal Nicaea isn't across the globe, or close to any great capitals of the world, but sits comfortably in southern Oklahoma. Its name is Camp Simpson, and it is the Boy Scout camp I spent a week at every summer as a teenager. Like Nicaea, it's off the beaten path, about forty miles from the interstate. Like Nicaea, it is situated on a peaceful lake, though with the decidedly less catchy name of Delaware Creek Reservoir 9. Like Nicaea did for the participants of its council, Camp Simpson offered me a place of contemplation and formation. And it was at Camp Simpson, my personal Nicaea, that I learned a lesson about what it means for God to be the Almighty.

It's been over fifteen years since I last visited Camp Simpson, but I still remember vividly a sign posted in the dining hall of the camp. There, on a simple typewritten page were unforgettable words of wisdom: "Before you tell God how big your problem is, tell the problem how big your God is!"

That tongue-in-cheek phrase has stuck with me. God is, as we've seen, the Almighty God who is high above it all. As one ancient prayer says, God is "uncontainable, of virtues indescribable, of greatness indefinable."[3] God was certainly larger than the problems of social awkwardness, one-sided romantic crushes, and midterms that

I faced when I first saw that sign at Camp Simpson. And God is still larger than my problems. Financial worries, parenting hurdles, and post-pandemic church leadership struggles cannot hold a candle to the Almighty God! Whatever problems you face similarly pale in the face of our very big God. This is not to say that family conflict, job loss, health problems, and addiction are trivial; they are just no match for our God.

But God is not just the Almighty; God is the Almighty Father. The truth is that you can also bring those problems to God, knowing that you will be seen, heard, and held. When it comes to the problems and trials of life, you are not alone. In your corner is your Almighty Father, whose "power at work within us is able to accomplish abundantly far more than all we can ask or imagine" (Ephesians 3:20). That's how big your God is. Remember that the next time a problem looks unsolvable or a challenge insurmountable.

Meet Your Maker

It is not enough to say that God is the Almighty. Plenty of other gods in the Egyptian, Greek, Roman, and other mythologies claimed impressive titles like this. One Roman god comes to mind, in particular. Jupiter was the Roman equivalent to the Greek god Zeus, and when the Romans built Jupiter a grand temple in Rome, they gave him a massive promotion. His temple was dedicated to Jupiter Optimus Maximus, or Jupiter Best and Greatest. The title, along with the imposing temple, was meant to instill in worshipers that Jupiter really was a god of immense power to be feared.

But not even this "best and greatest" god was thought to have made the earth, let alone the heavens. Romans didn't even believe Jupiter was immortal! At Nicaea, however, the council participants had searched the Scriptures and found verses like this,

We Believe in One God

*By the word of the L<small>ORD</small> the heavens were made
and all their host by the breath of his mouth.
He gathered the waters of the sea as in a bottle;
he put the deeps in storehouses.*

*Let all the earth fear the L<small>ORD</small>;
let all the inhabitants of the world stand in awe of him,
for he spoke, and it came to be;
he commanded, and it stood firm.*

(Psalm 33:6-9)

This God, our God, created the heavens and the earth by voice command alone. Far higher than any squabbles among the petty gods on Mount Olympus, the God of Israel reigns alone in power and ability.

And a tiny portion of "heaven and earth," of course, is you. God the Creator of heaven and earth is also *your* Maker. This is what Paul was getting at when he got up and preached in Athens about that "unknown god" altar mentioned above. He declared, "What therefore you worship as unknown, this I proclaim to you. The God who made the world and everything in it, he who is Lord of heaven and earth, does not live in shrines made by human hands.... 'For in him we live and move and have our being'" (Acts 17:23-24, 28).

Paul is contrasting the one God, the Maker of all things, with the gods that human hands have made. There is a word for worshiping something created instead of the Creator: idolatry. It is idolatry to trade your worship of something worthy, like the Maker of heaven and earth, for something that you can make with your own hands. In other words, if it didn't make you, it can't make you whole. We might not be tempted to worship the idols mentioned in Psalm 135 earlier in this chapter, but we are no less prone to idolatry. When we view idolatry not as simply worshiping an idol but instead as giving our ultimate allegiance to something other than God and finding our value in it, some common idols come into view.

Money is a perennial idol for many. If our self-worth is measured by the number at the bottom of our bank statements, we are likely giving money more worth than it is due. Politics is another pernicious idol. God has called us to be stewards of the earth, loving neighbors, and upstanding citizens. And in a democracy, that means voting and being politically active. The trap of idolatry springs when we define ourselves by our politics and confuse the success of our political party with the advancement of the reign of God.

The list of idols continues. Comfort, security, sports, and other people can all compete with God for our affection and attention. Most of these things are good gifts of God, things made by our Maker to bless or aid us. We go astray when we lose focus on the Creator in favor of the created. This was why it was important for the Council of Nicaea to establish that their one God was also the Maker worthy of worship.

The Creator and the Created

There is an old joke that goes something like this: A group of engineers make a scientific breakthrough. They can now make a human out of dirt! So they brag to God, "We can create life, just like you!" God responds, "Oh, really? Show me." So the engineers take some dirt, put it into their machine, and out comes a person. God laughs and says, "That's nice. Next time, use your own dirt."

Creatures can construct, compose, and even synthesize, but they cannot create. We talk about creating, and we prize "creativity" in students, but humanity cannot create in the way that God creates. We compose beautiful symphonies, but music existed long before the first concert hall opened. We construct magnificent skyscrapers, cathedrals, and palaces, but with preexistent materials. We conceive and deliver precious babies, and it is a wondrous miracle, but they, too, are grown with inherited genes and transferred nutrients. All these creative acts are done as extensions of our nature as image-bearers of God (Genesis 2; Psalm 8), but none of them involves creating something out of nothing.

This reminds me of an old neighbor of mine. Some years ago, I lived in a neighborhood with a very strict HOA, or homeowners association. Our grass couldn't get too long, but we couldn't mow it too low, either. Cars left parked on the street would be towed within twenty-four hours. One particular rule was that any fences in the neighborhood had to be made of "natural" materials, such as wood or stone. One weekend, though, my neighbor put up a white plastic vinyl fence. After several rounds of threatening letters from the HOA leadership, he showed up to a meeting to plead his case. My neighbor, it turned out, was a chemist, and he brought an analysis showing that the plastic from his fence was indeed made of "natural" materials, such as liquid natural gas and the element chlorine.

Whether because he convinced the HOA on the merits of his case or because his chemistry lesson bored them immensely, they let his fence stand. We don't have to understand the chemistry behind it to appreciate the truth my neighbor was getting at: all "man-made" products are actually just "natural" products humans have done something to. God has made everything that there is, or as the Nicene Creed puts it, "all that is, seen and unseen." From massive galaxies to the microscopic elements that made up my neighbor's fence, God has made it all.

Striking a Balance

Let's not lose the forest for the trees here. We've been looking at how the Nicene Creed opens and what it says about God the Father. This chapter opened by comparing the Nicene Creed to Christianity's "elevator pitch," which has to walk a fine line between saying enough to cover the necessary elements without being too long or getting bogged down in extraneous information. To go back to our central metaphor of the Nicene Creed as a map leading us to a deeper relationship with God, a map isn't any good if it doesn't have enough information. But by the same token, a map is useless if it is overcrowded.

So now that we've seen what the Nicene Creed says about God the Father, we can pause and ask: Does it say everything that needs to be said? Or could it go further and be more specific? This question will come up again as we consider different portions of the creed.

Think about it in terms of the different kinds of Christian friends many of us have. There are disagreements within church families, just like in regular families. I hope that my church never agrees on everything. What a boring church that would be! In my church, we have sisters and brothers with a wide range of beliefs on many issues. Some interpret the Book of Genesis literally and believe the Earth is around six thousand years old, while others believe it is the 4.5 billion years claimed by scientists. Some worshipers prefer the newer worship anthems written in this century; others claim a good hymn hasn't been written since the 1800s! The list of these differing opinions could take up several pages. Our pews are filled with differences of opinions like these, but they don't stop us from being faithful and friendly members of the same congregation.

Then there are those friends of ours who belong to other denominations. Friendships across denominations are of immense value to your faith; these friends stretch our faith and deepen our experience of God. Like I said in the opening of this book's introduction, I have close friends who are Roman Catholic, Anglican, Baptist, and nondenominational. We don't agree on everything, and some of the things we disagree on are very important to us! My Roman Catholic friends do not believe Holy Communion can be shared with people outside their denomination. As a Methodist who believes Christ has opened his table to all, this difference would keep me from worshiping fully with my Catholic friends. To take another example, my Southern Baptist friend believes that salvation is limited to a certain number of people God has already selected. My Methodist understanding of salvation leads me in a different direction, that salvation is open to all and is a choice enabled by grace.

> **Salvation is open to all and is a choice enabled by grace.**

I highlight these differences because they are real issues that separate denominations. And yet, we are all Christians still. Because the Nicene Creed bounds our faith, we are free to occupy different spaces and still recognize others as Christians. The creed was created as a perfectly balanced map. It said enough to lead us reliably to a truer and deeper relationship with God. And it also left enough blank spaces on the page to allow us to explore faithfully.

The Importance of Starting Strong

For this reason, it is helpful that the Nicene Creed did not immediately address the controversial matters for which the council had been called. Rather, it began on the firm foundation of God's oneness and omnipotence, to which every participant agreed. What we will consider in the next chapter, however, was much more divisive.

But before we turn the page on God the Father, it's worth pausing to reflect on how important this first portion is in its own right. The Nicene Creed reinforced that we believe in one, and only one, God who is the Almighty. Further, this one God is not off at a distance, having made heaven and earth and then taking a back seat. Rather, this almighty God is also the Father, who loves creation with a steadfast and incomparable love.

I experienced this in a striking way recently. One Sunday morning in the middle of a cold December, a teenager named Audrey showed up for worship and sat directly in front of the pulpit. Normally in my church's experience, teenagers don't show up on their own, let alone sit in the front row! After worship, Audrey told me that she was new to town, having been placed in a foster home a block from our church. She had never been to a church service before in her life. She knew nothing about God, but she told me that she needed something in her life and that religion might be it.

Audrey's life had been one of constant change and uncertainty. She started coming to church every time the doors were open, as soon as they were open. "When I'm here, I feel like a weight is off of my shoulders," she told me. Audrey needed to know that God is the Almighty; that though her life might seem constantly in flux, God stays the same. She found comfort in the truth that God could be for her a source of constancy and strong support. But at the same time, Audrey needed to know that God is her Father, too. God is her Father, immeasurably better than her biological father, wanting a relationship with her and desiring her flourishing. God is far above but never far off; these are the twin truths that made a world of difference in one teenager's life. There are people in your community, your neighborhood, your church, and maybe even your family who, like Audrey, need to hear these truths.

Our world has changed substantially since the time of the Council of Nicaea. Back then, in the 300s, insisting so forcefully as the creed does upon one God to the exclusion of all others marked the establishment of a firm boundary for Christianity. Roman emperors had claimed affinity with non-Roman gods in the past, as Emperor Constantine had done with the Christian God, and they had been assimilated quite well into the empire. No doubt many Romans would have been happy to incorporate this Yahweh, along with the god's powerful son, Jesus, into their panoply of deities. But at Nicaea, as the Church had already done at pivotal moments for its first three centuries, the leaders of Christianity refused to back down from their commitment to the worship of God alone.

Now, seventeen hundred years on from the council, the religious landscape is much changed. Instead of competing for space in a crowded marketplace of different gods, demigods, and Caesars-turned-god, Nicene Christianity now contends with a lack of faith in any god. While many people still report a connection or yearning for the spiritual, there is less interest in the personal God proclaimed in the creed. Compared to even a century ago, there is less knowledge about God among our neighbors. And yet, people like Audrey are still in search of the truth that the Nicene Creed proclaims.

The world changes, but the message of the Nicene Creed is the same. Like a good elevator pitch, these opening words of the creed pique our interest, hooking us into wanting to learn more about this God who loves us and is near to us. And it is in the person of Jesus Christ, whom the creed turns to next and is the focus of the next chapter, that we discover just how much God loves us and just how near to us God comes.

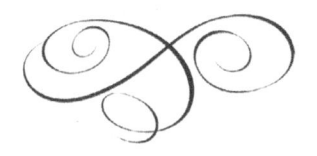

CHAPTER 2

Of One Being with the Father

We believe in one Lord, Jesus Christ,
the only Son of God,
eternally begotten of the Father,
God from God, Light from Light,
true God from true God,
begotten, not made,
of one Being with the Father;
through him all things were made.

Sloganeering

Slogans are everywhere in our world. There are slogans for companies and corporations, slogans for nonprofits, and slogans for political campaigns. If I were to sing a jingle that included the words, "I'm lovin' it," a pair of McDonald's golden arches would begin to glow in our heads. If I asked, "What's in your wallet?" many of us might hear it in the voice of the actor Samuel L. Jackson on behalf of Capital One. In my neck of the woods, it's just not Christmastime until we hear the jingle for Oklahoma City–based BC Clark Jewelers' annual anniversary sale.

Some of these slogans bury deeply into our minds, and even into our collective cultural memory. This is especially the case with political slogans. We might easily remember some of the slogans of political candidates in the past couple decades, but most people can still connect the slogan "I like Ike" to the campaign of President Dwight Eisenhower. I know that slogan, and I was born forty years after it debuted! Going back even further, some of us might have heard the election slogan "Tippecanoe and Tyler Too," but fewer remember that it originated in the presidential election of 1840 as a reference to future president William Henry Harrison and his running mate, John Tyler. President Harrison, "Old Tippecanoe," may have only served as president for thirty-one days, but his slogan has lived on for almost two hundred years!

Even nonprofits get in on the sloganeering action. The American Cancer Society's slogan is that they are The Official Sponsor of Birthdays, a poignant and heart-tugging slogan that opens the wallets of anyone wanting to help cancer patients have more birthdays. Closer to home for many of us, in 2001 The United Methodist Church adopted the slogan "Open hearts. Open minds. Open doors." Even though United Methodists haven't actively promoted that slogan in several years, it is still a memorable one that resonates. Why? Because it captures a compelling thought in a succinct and easy-to-repeat format, like all great slogans. In short, everyone loves a good slogan. And as we'll see, people will even love a bad slogan.

There Was When He Was Not

In the years before the Council of Nicaea, one such bad slogan was coined. It went like this: "There was when he was not." This catchy slogan (trust me, it was a lot catchier in its original Greek!) claimed that Jesus is not eternal like God the Father. Rather, the slogan claims, there was a time before Jesus existed. It was coined by a man named Arius, who was a priest in the city of Alexandria, Egypt, and has come down to us in history as the main antagonist at the Council of Nicaea.

Despite his reputation, Arius was a devoted and sincere man of faith who took very seriously the core tenets of Christianity. And as we saw in the last chapter, that includes a firm commitment to the existence of one and only one God. That God is unrivaled in power and authority, and that God made everything that there is. Unlike the Greek and Roman religions, there is no room in Christianity for competition with God.

What to do with Jesus, then? On the one hand, Jesus said things like, "The Father and I are one" (John 10:30). But on the other, he also claimed distance between himself and God the Father: "Why do you call me good? No one is good but God alone" (Luke 18:19). The issue of the incarnated Son of God presented a dilemma. Reconciling the seemingly contradictory positions of monotheism (belief in one God) and a divine Son was a full-time activity in the years before and after the Council of Nicaea. And the council's solution to this tension is the focus of this chapter.

For the priest Arius, he came down on what seemed to be the most faithful, God-honoring position: Jesus is indeed divine, but not in the same way as God the Father. Drawing on the familial stereotypes of Father and Son, Arius claimed the Son had to come later than the Father and was subordinate to him. That is, Jesus is divine, but in a derivative sense. And just as all earthly fathers existed before their children are born, so God the Father existed before the Son of God. This was, to Arius, the clearly superior theology, and he came up with a slogan to teach his people: "There was when he was not."

The "he" in that slogan refers to the Son, and Arius meant that there was some point in time when the Son did not exist but the Father did. This slogan, and its underlying assertions, caught like wildfire in Arius's hometown of Alexandria, one of the largest and most important cities in the Roman Empire. It continued to spread despite firm denunciations from Arius's bishop in Alexandria, a man (confusingly) named Alexander. At one point in the AD 320s, a full one-third of Alexander's priests opposed him and supported Arius.[1]

> **What the Nicene Creed says about Jesus can unlock for us a greater love of our Savior and a richer life of faith.**

This was the primary issue that led to the Council of Nicaea's convening. So as the participants wrote out their creed, after describing who God the Father is, they turned to define more fully who God the Son is. This chapter details that definition. Along the way, we'll see the importance and dangers of slogans and why it matters that Jesus is of one being with the Father. What the Nicene Creed says about Jesus can unlock for us a greater love of our Savior and a richer life of faith.

One Lord

The first thing the Nicene Creed says about Jesus is that he is our "one Lord." This might cause some confusion. As we saw in the previous chapter, the Old Testament uses the word *Lord* to refer to God the Father. Sometimes, as in the *Shema* declaration of Deuteronomy 6, it looks like LORD, as it is a shorthand for YHWH, the divine and unspeakable name of God given to Moses in Exodus 6. Over the centuries, faithful Jews began writing YHWH as *Adonai*, a Hebrew word for Lord, lest they accidentally try to pronounce the divine name. *Adonai* is then translated in the Bible as "Lord" with small caps to distinguish it with other instances of the word.

As the New Testament writers began to write their Gospels and Letters, however, Jesus became associated with the title Lord. In Paul's letters, it is something of a formula for him to begin with "Grace to you and peace from God our Father and the Lord Jesus Christ."[2] Jesus, whom John names as the "Word" at the beginning of his Gospel (John 1:1), became associated with the name of God. Thus, it is fitting to see Jesus as the Lord. But the creed goes one step further. Just as there is just one God, so there is just one Lord.

In the ancient world, lords were a dime a dozen. The words *adon* in Hebrew and *kurios* in Greek mean "lord," and they appear hundreds of times in the Bible. Many of those times, they don't mean "Lord," as in God, but are titles of respect for various people. Think of it like all the lords and ladies of medieval times, or how some of us teach our children to address people as "sir" or "ma'am." In the presence of a member of the aristocracy, royalty, or a government or military official, the correct term of respect would be "lord."

In that context, then, it was important to affirm that Jesus was not one lord of many, but the one Lord. The authors of the creed again reached back to Paul: "As in fact there are many gods and many lords—yet for us there is one God, the Father, from whom are all things and for whom we exist, and one Lord, Jesus Christ" (1 Corinthians 8:5-6). One God and one Lord, Father and Son.

Who's the Boss?

There is a deep implication for our lives in this declaration that Jesus is the Lord. This is because the statement "Jesus is Lord" has two necessary corollaries. The first is this: Jesus is Lord, so Caesar is not. That is, if Jesus is our Lord, then he is the supreme authority for our lives, not any earthly political power. The Nicene Creed gets political here, making it clear that all Christians are ultimately citizens of the emerging kingdom of God who recognize Christ as Lord. We are all citizens of that kingdom first, before we are citizens of whatever state, country, kingdom, or empire we find ourselves in.

There are times when this political statement causes hardship for Christians. That was certainly the case for some of the participants of the Council of Nicaea. As we noted in the introduction, the Church had faced severe persecution just a generation before the council convened. As a powerful illustration of this, sitting in attendance at the council was a bishop named Paphnutius whose eye had been removed during that persecution. Other martyrs throughout history have faced similar fates or worse for their commitment to Christ.

For Christians today, especially those in the United States, we likely won't face anything so gruesome. But the declaration "Jesus is Lord, so Caesar is not" still reorients us. It tells us not to hold too tightly to our political, national, or civic identities. Politics is important, and being a citizen of your nation is a blessing, but they pale in comparison to our ultimate allegiance to Jesus. Our faith should inform our politics, not the other way around.

The second corollary to the declaration "Jesus is Lord" is this: Jesus is Lord, so I am not. This one might be harder to swallow. We like to think of ourselves as in control and in charge of our lives, but to be a Christian is to acknowledge that Jesus is the Lord of our life. Just like the medieval lords who directed the actions and lives of their subjects, so our Lord directs our lives. The difference, of course, between earthly lords and the Lord Jesus is that Jesus is gracious and always good. The truth remains, though, that following Jesus means subjecting ourselves to his lordship.

Methodists have reminded ourselves of this from time to time by praying a prayer written by John Wesley, the founder of Methodism.

We do this in my church at the beginning of every new year in what's called our Covenant Renewal Service. It might be my favorite day on the church calendar; the service is just that powerful. If you've never been part of a service like this, ask your pastor to consider it next January. The central prayer in that service, Wesley's Covenant Prayer, reinforces the point we're making, as the prayer begins, "I am no longer my own, but thine." We go on to ask that our Lord uses us how he chooses, praying, "I freely and heartily yield all things to thy pleasure and disposal." We pray, and pray boldly, that we would not be in charge of our lives, but that God would.

This has profound implications for our everyday lives. If I were the one calling the shots in my life and I only had to worry about myself and the people I liked, I don't know how generous I would be. I certainly wouldn't be tithing 10 percent of my paycheck to the church when I could just pocket all the money myself! I probably wouldn't volunteer at my local food pantry, help pay strangers' utility bills, or package meals to deliver around the world if Jesus weren't calling the shots. But then, too, if Jesus weren't in control of my life, I would probably be more anxious, have a quicker temper, and have less motivation. In short, I'm a more generous person, a calmer parent, and altogether happier and more fulfilled, all precisely because Jesus is Lord, and I am not.

And speaking of Jesus, let's now turn to what the Nicene Creed says about the name "Jesus Christ."

Jesus the Christ, the Son of God

We see the words "Jesus Christ" together so often that many of us tend to think of Christ as Jesus's last name. But *Christ* is a Greek word for a specific title given to Jesus. *Christos* is a Greek word that means the same as the Hebrew word *mashiach*, which is usually transliterated as "Messiah." Both words literally mean "anointed one," a person chosen by God for a special purpose.

In the Old Testament, kings, priests, and prophets were all anointed with oil. The prophet Samuel, in selecting the young David to be king in Israel, "took the horn of oil and anointed him in the presence of his brothers, and the spirit of the LORD came mightily upon David from that day forward" (1 Samuel 16:13). Further back in Exodus, Moses is given instruction from the Lord to consecrate his brother, Aaron, and Aaron's sons as priests by anointing them with the same oil used to consecrate the ark of the covenant and other holy items (Exodus 30:22-33).

Several people, then, were chosen as christs, or messiahs, throughout Scripture. This includes heroes of the faith like David and Aaron, as well as some of the less faithful kings of Israel and Judah. At one point, a foreign king is even named by the Lord as among the anointed, a messiah. Isaiah 45 says of Cyrus, king of the Persian Empire:

> *Thus says the LORD to his anointed [messiah], to Cyrus,*
>   *whose right hand I have grasped*
>
> *. . . . .*
>
> *For the sake of my servant Jacob*
>   *and Israel my chosen,*
> *I call you by your name;*
>   *I give you a title, though you do not know me.*
>   *(vv. 1, 4)*

Over time, however, the Scriptures began to point to a single, ultimate messiah. This capital *M* Messiah would be the one who would fulfill all God's promises. This is who Isaiah refers to when he prophesies, "The spirit of the Lord GOD is upon me because the LORD has anointed me" (61:1).

> **Jesus is not only the Christ, God's chosen, but he is also the Son of God.**

In the New Testament, the people around Jesus discover that he is the Messiah, or Christ, at different speeds. John the Baptist, from King Herod's prison cell, sends his disciples to ask Jesus, "Are you the one who is to come, or are we to wait for another?" (Matthew 11:3) A few chapters later, Peter, filled with knowledge from above, declares to Jesus that he is "the Messiah, the Son of the living God" (Matthew 16:16). This is what it means for Jesus to be the Christ. He is not only the Christ, God's chosen, but he is also the Son of God. And to be a Son, there is a relationship to the Father that needs to be explored.

Begetting and Begotten

To explain this relationship between Father and Son, the Nicene Creed uses a term that has fallen out of use in the twenty-first century. The Son, they declared, is "eternally begotten of the Father." *Beget* is the term to describe when a man has a child (men *beget* their children; women *bear* them). Outside of Scripture, the term has all but been forgotten. To refresh yourself, reach for the nearest King James Version and read the thirty-nine "begats" of Jesus's genealogy in Matthew 1:1-16. That's almost 2.5 "begats" per verse!

It was critical, though, to describe the relationship of the Son to the Father in this way. The Son is distinct from the Father, so some kind of description is needed. But the Son is not part of the created universe made by the "maker of heaven and earth," so it is not accurate to say that Jesus was created or made. Instead, the authors of the creed reached to Scripture to find the language they needed.

The second psalm, subtitled in the NRSVue as "God's Promise to His Anointed [or Messiah]," has a depiction of the Father's relationship to the Christ:

> *I will tell of the decree of the* LORD:
> *He said to me, "You are my son;*
> *today I have begotten you."*
>   *(Psalm 2:7)*

This verse is quoted three times in the New Testament, once in Acts and twice in Hebrews. Each of these instances is explaining the relation of Jesus to God. Hebrews 1:5 explicitly quotes Psalm 2:7 to assert that Jesus is higher even than the angels, those created, heavenly beings.

The word used in the Nicene Creed for the "only" or "only begotten" portion referring to Jesus is the Greek word *monogenes*. It has the sense of "onlyborn," similar to referring to an oldest child as firstborn. *Monogenes* itself has deep scriptural roots, being found in both John 1 and John 3. In John 1, the Gospel writer is poetically describing the Incarnation as he says, "And the Word became flesh and lived among us, and we have seen his glory, the glory as of a father's only son [*monogenes*]" (v. 14). In John 3, we find it hidden in the Gospel's most well-known verse: "For God so loved the world that he gave his only [*monogenes*] Son" (v. 16).

But what does it mean that Jesus is "eternally" begotten? In essence, it means that Jesus was begotten from the Father in eternity, that is, outside of time. A more literal translation of the original Greek of the Nicene Creed is something like "begotten from the Father *before all ages*." That is, Jesus was born before time began. Before the modern age, before the Age of Enlightenment, before the Stone Age, before the Jurassic Era, before Genesis 1:1, Christ was begotten from the Father. This phrase "eternally begotten of the Father" explicitly contradicts the heretical slogan from Arius that we encountered at the beginning of the chapter. To say that Jesus was begotten of the Father before time means that Arius's phrase "There was when he was not" is flat-out wrong. As it turns out, there was not when he was not.

God from God

We've just been in the weeds of the Hebrew and Greek in the last couple sections, so let's take a breather with something we all enjoy: Christmas. Are you reading this chapter in the middle of spring or the heat of summer? Doesn't matter; it's never too early to think about Christmas!

One of my favorite Christmas hymns is "O Come, All Ye Faithful." The melody is forceful, the chorus is yearning and wishful, and its message is timeless. But like most Christmas carols, people tend only to remember the first verse. It's in the second verse, though, where the real beauty of the hymn lies. If it's hard to remember, here's the verse:

> True God of true God, Light from Light Eternal,
> lo, he shuns not the Virgin's womb;
> Son of the Father, begotten, not created.

This verse could have come straight out of Nicaea! We see not only the claim that Jesus is "begotten, not created," but we also find the next few lines of the creed. Jesus is "God from God, Light from Light, true God from true God."

The repetition in these lines is helpful. Three times in quick succession, with two of the times being nearly identical, the truth is reinforced that Jesus is God. Those at the council who subscribed to Arius's teachings would have had no problem saying that Jesus is "from God." Everything, as established in the first portion of the creed, is "from God." But Jesus is not just "from God" like you and I are. Jesus is "God from God." Begotten, yes, but still God.

To say that Jesus is "Light from Light" draws on some illuminating verses in Scripture. The psalmist says that "the Lord is my light and my salvation" (27:1) and "for with you is the fountain of life; / in your light we see light" (36:9). Hebrews 1 connects that light to Jesus, saying that "the Son is the light of God's glory and the imprint of God's being" (v. 3, CEB). Finally, John describes Jesus as "the true light, which enlightens everyone" (1:9). John also gives us the basis for referring to Jesus as "true God from true God." In 1 John 5:20, he writes of Jesus, "he is the true God and eternal life." Each of these appellations, God, Light, and true God, serve to close the distance in our minds between the Father and the Son. While it was tempting for early Christians to imagine that Jesus was a man who became divine, like so many earthly rulers had claimed of themselves, the truth revealed by the Holy Spirit was that Jesus is and always has been fully divine.

The Church's First Attack Ad

We started the chapter with a discussion of effective slogans and ads. Just as effective as positive slogans, though, are attack ads. Anyone who remembers President Lyndon Johnson's "Daisy" attack ad against his 1964 opponent Barry Goldwater can testify to this. (If you have never seen it, look it up sometime. It was pulled after airing only once for being too far over the line, but that one time was enough to make an impact.) Any time someone can smear their opponent with a catchy, incisive attack ad, it tends to stick in people's minds.

That is exactly what Arius did in the run-up to the Council of Nicaea. We have already dealt with the council's pushback against Arius's heretical slogan "there was when he was not." But now, with the clause "of one being with the Father," the crux of the matter comes to the fore. This is the chief reason for which the Council had been convened. At stake is our understanding of who Jesus is and, by extension, what his life, death, and resurrection mean for us.

The controversy before the Council of Nicaea between Arius and his bishop, Alexander, dealt with the "being," or nature, of Jesus. In

Of One Being with the Father

Greek, that word for being or nature is *ousia*. Arius was firm that, in order to preserve the truth that there is only one God, Jesus the Son could not have the same *ousia* as God the Father. At best, he could have a similar nature, but not an identical one. Ever the sloganeer, he attempted to smear Alexander by staking his position out for him. Arius launched the first attack ad in church history, claiming that Alexander believed that Jesus was *homoousios*, or "of one nature or being," with God. The idea was that such a thought would be so scandalous, so beyond the pale, that Alexander would be defamed by being anywhere near the term.

But as has happened more than once throughout church history, the attack ad backfired. Alexander, no unsavvy operator in his own right, took the bull by the horns. When the council convened at Nicaea, Alexander led the charge to insert the word *homoousios* into the creed. Such is the scandal of the gospel. As Paul would say, a scandal and foolishness to the world (1 Corinthians 1:23).

Smears like this have a tendency of being turned on their head in the Church. The origin of the term "Christian" to describe us was originally intended as a slur. "Little Christs" is what it literally means, as the Romans looked at the followers of Christ and sneered that they were just pretending to be "little Christs." But in the upside-down world of Christ's kingdom, being a "little Christ" is the highest honor we could have! *Methodists* has the same history. The earliest Methodists, John and Charles Wesley and their college buddies at Oxford, took their faith very seriously. They woke up early to pray and read Scripture, they practiced accountability, and they visited the sick and the imprisoned. Their peers, deriding the extreme "methodical" nature of their faith, labeled them "Methodists." And the name stuck.

Alexander attempted to do the same thing with the *homoousios* of Arius's attack ad. With the attempt, the Council of Nicaea waded into a theological and semantic debate that hinged on a single letter.

We Believe

The Power of a Single Letter

Words are powerful things. Sometimes, there is a world of difference between very similar words. A few letters can completely alter the intended meaning. A little while back, a Pizza Hut in Ontario found this out the hard way. One afternoon, they had to close their dining room due to unforeseen circumstances. So like any good restaurant, they put a sign on the door to let customers know. Only, they made an unfortunate typo. Instead of writing, "Due to unforeseen circumstances, the dining room is closed," they wrote, "Due to unforeseen circumcisions, the dining room is closed." Very regrettable, indeed.

Sometimes, all it takes is a single letter. A local Days Inn hotel recently tried to advertise their various amenities on their roadside letterboard sign, such as an indoor pool, hot tub, continental breakfast, and free WIFI. But instead of WIFI, they wrote "WIFE." Days Inns, apparently, are in the marriage business, and on the cheap!

The debate at Nicaea on the nature of Jesus also hinged on a single letter, though to less humorous effect. Alexander's opponents, put on the back foot by his championing of *homoousios*, sought a compromise. What if, they offered, we say that Jesus is of "similar" nature to the Father? In Greek, that would be the term *homoiousios*. If it's difficult to see in the dense pack of vowels in the middle of the term, there is an extra *i* (the Greek letter *iota*) added.

A few practical examples can help us see the distinction between *homoousios* and *homoiousios*. Every fall, my family likes to go apple picking at a nearby apple orchard and pumpkin picking at a nearby patch. (Personally, I don't see the appeal of paying extra to pick the apples myself compared to buying them from a grocery store, but I digress.) The word *homoousios* would describe two apples picked from the same tree. They might not be perfectly identical, but they are

Of One Being with the Father

the same in every way that counts. *Homoiousios*, then, would describe comparing an apple with a pumpkin. They share some similarities. They are both produce, both hand-picked, both have a protective layer with seeds inside, and both can be baked into delicious pies. But are they identical? Absolutely not. Try turning an apple into a jack-o-lantern and get back to me!

Here's another example: we could say that my old college intramural football team is *homoiousios* with the Kansas City Chiefs. Sure, there are similarities: a football, a roster of players, and a playbook. But it would be insulting in the extreme to tell Super Bowl MVP Patrick Mahomes that he and I are the same. I'd have a better chance saying my intramural team is *homoousios* with my beloved, long-suffering Chicago Bears, but that's a tangent for another day.

While not appearing in Scripture, *homoousios* is deeply resonant with it. (And for the record, *homoiousios* isn't in Scripture, either.) A few of Paul's words are helpful. Philippians 2:6, which begins what many consider to be the oldest hymn of the Church, says that Christ "existed in the form of God" and had "equality with God." Colossians 1:19 says that "for in him [Jesus], all the fullness of God was pleased to dwell." Not some of the fullness of God, all the fullness. Not a similar nature, the same nature. Not *homoiousios*, but *homoousios*.

> **There is not one iota of difference in the natures of the Father and the Son.**

When comparing those two terms, one a bold claim of faith and the other a heretical compromise, it is fascinating to note that only one letter, one *iota* separates them. But in that slight change is a monumental distinction. Because there is not one iota of difference in the natures of the Father and the Son.

A Quick Word on Heretics

Before we leave Arius behind, his reputation could use a little rehabilitation. Because he was on the losing side of the Council of Nicaea, history has not been kind to him. His name has been lent to a term, Arianism, which has been trotted out ever since to demean anyone who gets close to endorsing his heretical beliefs.

It needs to be said, then, that Arius was not trying to lead the Church astray with false teachings. Arius, as we've discussed, was a faithful man trying to make the faith understandable for those in his flock. Arius was earnestly and honestly trying to make sense of his faith for others. To be sure, the beliefs he advocated for were incorrect and thus correctly labeled "heretical." When presented with the tension of believing in one God and yet having a fully divine Son at the same time, he eased that tension by demoting Jesus. Wrong teaching? Absolutely. Done maliciously? Not a chance.

The same is true for any heresies we might confront today. People who are "heretics," or hold false beliefs, didn't adopt those false beliefs so they could hurt the Church. (For the record, people who turn against the faith are better called "apostates.") And besides, some people throw around the term "heresy" much too casually. Heresies are reserved for false beliefs opposed to core doctrines of Christianity, like those given in the Nicene Creed. Differences of opinion on Communion, baptism, and how to approach Scripture are not heresies, even if they're "wrong."

If you do happen to come upon a heretic at some point, here's how to handle it. First off, don't call them a "heretic" (they generally don't like that!). Rather, get to the bottom of how they arrived at the position they did. Most of the time, it came out of trying to ease some tension in our faith. So, with a spirit of gentleness (Galatians 6:1), guide them back to the correct understanding.

I have a soft spot for heretics because I used to be one. Well, I was as a kid, if only for a few days. As a teenager, I started reading the Bible on my own. And like not a few people, I seemed to see a stark difference between how God is presented in the Old Testament and subsequently in the New Testament. God in the Old Testament seemed bent on floods, plagues, and punishment. God in the New Testament, though, was all about love. It seemed to be that, at best, God changed or, at worst, there were two different Gods. Luckily, I brought this concern to my youth pastor, and he graciously and patiently set me straight. I've been good to go ever since, as I've seen more and more how God in the Old Testament is still grace-filled and abounding in steadfast love.

The Limits of Scripture

Before arriving at the end of our discussion on the nature of Jesus, it is helpful to reflect on what we have just witnessed. At the Council of Nicaea, the preeminent leaders of the Church in 325 arrived at a new level of clarity about God the Son. Jesus is of one being (*homoousios*) with the Father. But to make that clarification, they used a word not found anywhere in Scripture.

The same can be said of the doctrine of the Trinity. Try as you might, you will not find the word *Trinity* in your Bible. Those words, *homoousios* and Trinity, developed over the course of the Church's first few centuries. And while they certainly have support in Scripture, they are not plainly found there. Hence the controversies surrounding Arius and others. They looked, and looked faithfully, at the same Scriptures, yet they came to different conclusions.

This issue highlights the limits of Scripture. Please don't get me wrong here: Scripture is the primary way God has communicated with us. One of the Articles of Religion of my faith tradition makes clear:

"The Holy Scripture containeth all things necessary to salvation."[3] But if you insist that God is three Persons, or that the Father and Son share one nature, then you have reached the limits of Scripture.

So thanks be to God that God has given us more than Scripture alone! We stand as the inheritors of a rich tradition, which includes not only Scripture but also creeds like the Nicene Creed as well as the early liturgy, teachers, and leaders of the Church.[4] Consider this: we know that the Bible did not descend as an already-compiled book from heaven. Rather, it was written by God-inspired people over several centuries. Then, after the last book was written, it took a few centuries to coalesce into what we call the Old and New Testaments. Floating around the books of the New Testament were other Letters, Gospels, and other writings that were used in churches but ultimately didn't make the cut. The list, or *canon*, of New Testament books was finally agreed upon at the Council of Carthage in AD 397.

That means that the Nicene Creed, adopted at the Council of Nicaea in 325, predates the "official" New Testament by almost seventy-five years! While this does not mean that the Nicene Creed is better or more authoritative for us than Scripture, it does point to this larger truth: we don't worship the Bible.

We worship God—a God, we believe, who sent the Holy Spirit to enliven and guide the Church. In the same century that the Holy Spirit was inspiring the Church to assemble the New Testament as we know it, that same Spirit was also inspiring the Church to adopt the Nicene Creed.

This gets to the heart of why the Nicene Creed is important not only as a historical document but also for our faith today. In recovering an appreciation for the whole heritage of faith, we see an increased value of the Nicene Creed, which developed alongside Scripture itself. By adopting and often reciting the creed, our faith is made alive. Like the participants at Nicaea, we are awakened by the Holy Spirit to see truths that are in Scripture but might not be obvious there. The Nicene Creed, alongside Scripture, becomes the bedrock of an enlivened faith that can meet the challenges of the twenty-first century. Ignoring or shunning the creed is like shutting off a burner on your stove. You can still cook a good meal with the other burner, but you're missing out on additional power and heat!

The Full Effect

As this chapter has laid out, a cornerstone of our faith embedded in the Nicene Creed is that Jesus is fully God and of one being with the Father. This foundational doctrine was not made flippantly or for purely semantic reasons. There was a reason, a deep and transformative reason, that people like Alexander fought so vigorously against Arius and his attempts to demote Jesus to some lesser status. This reason makes all the difference in our lives and salvation.

Think about it: If Jesus were not fully God, then what would have been accomplished in his life, death, and resurrection? If Jesus is only partially God, then we are only partially saved, partially restored, partially reborn.

> **We are fully saved, fully restored, fully reborn, because Jesus our Lord and Savior is also fully God.**

But we are not partially saved. We are fully saved, fully restored, fully reborn, because Jesus our Lord and Savior is also fully God. Paul wrote in Galatians 4,

> *But when the fullness of time had come, God sent his Son ... in order to redeem those who were under the law, so that we might receive adoption as children. And because you are children, God has sent the*

Spirit of his Son into our hearts, crying, "Abba! Father!" So you are no longer a slave but a child, and if a child then also an heir through God.
(Galatians 4:4-7)

We are children and heirs of God because Jesus, God's own Son and fully God himself, has redeemed us. Not partial adoption, but full adoption and full redemption. As the hymn "I Surrender All," written by a Methodist named Judson Van DeVenter, boasts in its final verse:

All to Jesus, I surrender;
now I feel the sacred flame.
O the joy of full salvation!
Glory, glory to his name!

It is a joy-filled, glorious, full salvation that is brought by Jesus. And this full salvation is accomplished not by our own efforts but in surrendering those efforts to the Son of God, who has already accomplished it for us.

This opens an incredible door for our faith. In those times that we feel hopeless, abandoned, or alone, we can remember that Jesus hasn't left us. When feelings of failure or inadequacy haunt us, we can remember that our salvation is effective because it is brought by someone who is fully God. The bridge back to God wasn't started on our end but on God's. Now, we turn to the next portion of the creed to see how and why that bridge was built.

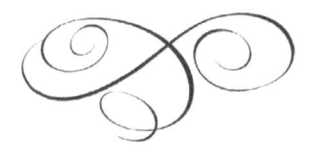

CHAPTER 3

For Us and for Our Salvation

For us and for our salvation
he came down from heaven,
was incarnate of the Holy Spirit and the Virgin Mary
and became truly human.
For our sake he was crucified under Pontius Pilate;
he suffered death and was buried.

The Reason for the Season

We have spent two chapters on twelve lines of the Nicene Creed, discussing the bedrock of what Christians believe about God the Father and God the Son. Important claims have been made, lines drawn, and distinctions clarified:

How many Gods are there? One.

What did that one God make? Everything.

Is the Son of God eternal? Yes.

Is the Son fully divine? One hundred percent.

We Believe

Now, however, the creed gets personal. It gets personal not only in pivoting to the biographical details of God the Son's earthly life, but personal also for those reciting the creed. Because before any of those biographical details are shared, the Council of Nicaea makes clear: it all happened "for us and for our salvation."

Every Christmas season, there is a certain amount of handwringing that goes on. Amid all the commercialization that has hijacked the holidays, people like to break out a gently chiding rhyme: "Remember the reason for the season!" The reason, of course, is the birth of Jesus to Mary on that dark, Bethlehem night, when God moved from infinite to infant. And when there are flashy sales at car dealerships and department stores, we tend to lose sight of this reason. When retailers gained the ability to send sale notifications to our phones instantly, all hope seemed lost.

> **Reminders about the true meaning of Christmas are always welcome.**

Reminders, then, about the true meaning of Christmas are always welcome. But the Nicene Creed takes "the reason for the season" a step further. Jesus came down from heaven and was born to Mary, the creed says, not for an abstract or unknown reason. Rather, he came *for us*. He came *for our salvation*. Driving the point further, the council used a form of the word *our* in Greek that connotes added emphasis.[1] This unusual and emphatic word heightens the good news proclaimed in the creed: he came for *our* salvation. Ours!

St. Athanasius, who was a young participant of the Council of Nicaea and went on to become the Nicene Creed's greatest defender, reflected on the purpose of Jesus's incarnation. He wrote pointedly, "For *we* were the purpose of his embodiment, and for *our* salvation he so loved human beings as to come to be and appear in a human body."[2] So as we trace the details of Jesus's life, death, and resurrection, keep in mind that all of it was for you and for your salvation.

The Incarnation

As we have seen already, the authors of the Nicene Creed relied on the opening of the Gospel of John to describe Jesus. It was from John 1:14 that they borrowed language of Jesus being the only-begotten Son of God the Father. "And the Word became flesh and lived among us, and we have seen his glory, the glory as of a father's only son." At the beginning of that sentence, they then found the words to describe how the Son came down from heaven.

Jesus "became flesh," John says. In Latin, the word for flesh is *carnis*, which gives the sense not only of flesh but also meat (hence carnivores that eat meat). So, when Jesus stepped down from heaven and into flesh, he was in-carn-ated. This Incarnation was the event when God revealed himself in a manifestly real way. Eugene Peterson put it beautifully and concretely in *The Message* translation of John 1:14, which says, "The Word became flesh and blood, and moved into the neighborhood."

No longer would God be at a distance or hidden from our sight. Where Moses had to turn his face to avoid seeing God directly, now God can be seen, felt, and even cradled. There are many aspects of what Jesus's life, death, and resurrection accomplished for us, which the Nicene Creed covers, but the first one is that Jesus's incarnation gives us a better, more complete view of God. You could say that with the Incarnation, Jesus is God fleshed out for us.

This Incarnation was accomplished by two agents. Just as each of us was conceived by two parents, so, too, were two involved in the Incarnation: the Holy Spirit and Mary. By including the partnership of Mary and the Holy Spirit in Jesus's conception, the creed draws in the account of Jesus's birth found in Luke's Gospel. In Luke 1, when the angel Gabriel announces to an astonished Mary that she will bear "the Son of the Most High" (v. 32), he explains that this will happen because "the Holy Spirit will come upon you." "Therefore," Gabriel says, "the child to be born will be holy; he will be called Son of God" (v. 35).

How can this happen? How could God be born as a human baby? This is the definition of a miracle, something that makes no sense, has no precedent, and yet happens without natural explanation. The poet W. H. Auden, in his excellent Advent poem *For the Time Being*, puts it powerfully:

> How could the Eternal do a temporal act,
> The Infinite become a finite fact?[3]

Auden expresses the incredulity and wonder many of us feel; how did God do this? The Incarnation is a miracle, plain and simple. And it established a bridge that reunited us with God.

Bridging the Gap

In the world of civil engineering that I inhabited before following a call to ministry, the bridge designers were the cool kids. Within the hierarchy of civil engineers who design roads, highways, airports, water and sewer systems, and bridges, it is the bridge engineers who are the rock stars. Why is this the case? Who knows! Is it weird to imagine that some civil engineers are cooler than others? Probably!

In a college internship one summer, I had a chance to work with my company's esteemed bridge design team. In that time, I got to see how bridges were designed and built. Imagine, for a minute, a wide canyon that needs to be spanned by a bridge. Once all the plans are done and printed, the materials ordered, and the contractors hired,

For Us and for Our Salvation

how do you decide from which side of the canyon to start building? It's a trick question: the answer is both sides. Teams start working from both sides, spanning the chasm, until the sides meet in the middle and the bridge is completed.

When we talk about Jesus bridging the gap between Heaven and Earth, between God and humanity, this is what we mean. Throughout history, God has been reaching down to us, seeking to undo the separation wrought by sin. But because of that sin, we have been unable to reach up and bridge the gap. The Incarnation, then, is God taking on human form to build the bridge reliably from our side. In this metaphor, Jesus is the ultimate bridge engineer. (I hope there aren't any bridge engineers reading this book; they don't need the ego boost!) When the chasm seemed far too wide, and every attempt of ours to build a bridge back to God had failed, Jesus was born to start the construction from both sides.

The reason bridges are built from both sides is because the midpoint of the bridge is the most precarious, being the furthest from either side. It takes careful attention and intense precision to make the sides meet perfectly in the middle. Luckily, the bridge that I designed was short, so the stakes were much lower. For the record, the bridge I designed is the one that spans the Barron Fork Creek on State Highway 51 about fifteen miles east of Tahlequah, Oklahoma. You can drive across it, but I'd do it quickly! Even more luckily for all of us, Jesus is a much stronger and more trustworthy bridge than any built by an engineer. He is a sure and certain bridge to reunite us with God, precisely because he is the only one who could build it from both sides.

A Particular Scandal

There is a scandal lurking in the claims the Gospels make about the birth of Jesus. It is not just that God has entered the human story to bring salvation; it's also that God has entered it at a specific time, in a specific place, with a specific person. Consider the opening of Luke 2, recited at Christmas pageants the world over:

> *In those days a decree went out from Caesar Augustus that all the world should be registered. This was the first registration and was taken while Quirinius was governor of Syria. All went to their own towns to be registered. Joseph also went from the town of Nazareth in Galilee to Judea, to the city of David called Bethlehem, because he was descended from the house and family of David.*
>
> *(vv. 1-4)*

Luke is putting down historical and geographical markers here. For the historical, the Incarnation happened at a specific time: during the reign of Caesar Augustus in Rome and the governorship of Quirinius in Syria. In the previous chapter, Luke includes that this happens when Herod was king of Judea. With each of these, there is a tightening of the focus, from the world-ruling Caesar Augustus, to the provincial bureaucrat Quirinius, to the client king Herod, then to a simple carpenter from Nazareth and his bride-to-be.

There are geographical markers, too. The scope narrows from Rome, center of the world, to the small village of Bethlehem on the outskirts of Jerusalem. At each step, God homes in on a particular place, at a particular time, and a particular person. Theologians have called the focus on particulars like this the "scandal of particularity." It's a scandal because it seems so ludicrous for God (who is the creator of heaven and earth, remember) to be so focused on and limited to something so particular.

This scandal began all the way back in the first book of the Bible. There, in Genesis 12, God chose Abraham to become a great nation. God declared, "I will make of you a great nation, and I will bless you and make your name great, so that you will be a blessing. I will bless those who bless you, and the one who curses you I will curse, and in you all the families of the earth shall be blessed" (vv. 2-3). Throughout the Old Testament, God uses this particular people to accomplish God's purposes and to carry the truth. God makes covenants with successive generations of this people, first with Abraham, then Jacob, then Moses, then David, in the process refining his love for this particular people.

This refining comes to a head with the Incarnation. C. S. Lewis, the great author and theologian, put this process of refining poignantly: "The process grows narrower and narrower, sharpens at last into one small bright point like the head of a spear. It is a Jewish girl at her prayers. All humanity has narrowed to that."[4] Mary, this Jewish girl, will bear the one in whom all the love of God is focused. But the particularity of Jesus's existence is not just for one person, or even for one people, but for everyone. It is as God told Abraham when the scandal began: "In you all the families of the earth shall be blessed." With this, having established how the Son of God was born, by Mary and the Spirit, the Nicene Creed has one last point to reiterate on Jesus's humanity.

Among Us

As I write this, there is a popular computer game among the youth of my church. It's called *Among Us*, and the premise is a fun and simple take on classic "whodunit" games like *Clue* or *Mafia*. All of the participants play as astronauts on a spaceship. But there's a catch: there is an impostor among us (hence the title). This Impostor might look like the others, but they are not one of the good guys. The Impostor is causing mischief, dismantling parts of the spaceship and taking other astronauts out of commission. The other players must figure out which one is the Impostor before it is too late.

Among Us is a great game that teaches players the benefits of teamwork and the limitations of assumptions. I may have spent more than a couple hours playing the game conducting "research" for this chapter! I bring it up, though, because there was a certain group of people in the run-up to the Council of Nicaea that thought of Jesus exactly like the Impostor in *Among Us*.

Docetism was a heresy that had been brewing for over a century by the time the council met in Nicaea. It took its name from the Greek word that means "to appear" or "to seem." The name stuck because Docetists claimed that Jesus was only divine, and not human at all. He only *seemed* human. Like Arius's heresy of not believing Jesus was fully divine, Docetism was a well-meaning heresy. To Docetists, it was unconscionable that God would subject himself to being confined to humanity. It was scandalous to think that he got hungry, felt pain, and went through puberty. And it was downright offensive to imagine that God would actually suffer and die on a Roman torture device.

Their solution, then, was that Jesus's humanity was simply an illusion. John's claim that "the Word became flesh" in the poetic opening chapter of his Gospel was just that, poetry. The Docetists' solution was a sanitized, safe way to read the Gospels without being confronted by the unprecedented claim that God would actually become human. From the safety of this heresy, Jesus was no more human than the Impostor in a round of *Among Us* is a real member of the crew.

Fully, Truly Human

But of course, Jesus was actually human. Jesus was not an impostor among us but incarnate for us. Several points in Scripture make this clear. In addition to John's claim about the Word becoming flesh in his Gospel, he repeats the sentiment in his letters. He writes, "By this you know the Spirit of God: every spirit that confesses that Jesus

Christ has come in the flesh is from God" (1 John 4:2). The author of Hebrews at several points asserts Jesus's humanity. Written in the style of a lengthy and rich sermon, Hebrews claims, "Since, therefore, the children share flesh and blood, he himself likewise shared the same things" (2:14). Going further, "Therefore he had to become like his brothers and sisters in every respect, so that he might become a merciful and faithful high priest in the service of God" (2:17).

> **Jesus was not an impostor among us but incarnate for us.**

This next clause in the creed reminds us that Jesus "became truly human." In the last chapter, we saw the great lengths the Council of Nicaea went to in securing the divinity of Jesus. Jesus was "true God from true God" and "of one Being with the Father." This was necessary to combat the heresy being spread by Arius, who insisted that Jesus was not fully divine. Here, in the section concerning Jesus's incarnation, the council's participants similarly stressed his humanity. They did so to confront the Docetists.

What's more, the Gospel writers also include several scenes of Jesus having all manner of physical experiences. At various points, he weeps, feels weariness, is hungry, and thirsts (John 11:35; 4:6; Matthew 4:2; and John 19:28, respectively). Then, when the risen Christ appears to his disciples, he still bears the wounds from the cross (John 20:24-29). Again, St. Athanasius summarizes it well: "As he became human, it is proper for these things to be said of him as human, that he might be shown possessing a real and not illusory body."[5] Add all of this up, and it is clear that Jesus, while fully God, was also fully and truly human.

Speaking of adding things up, this dual truth of Jesus's divinity and humanity has caused no small amount of confusion. It may be fairly obvious that you and I are both 100 percent human. It is also reasonable to say that God the Father is 100 percent divine. But how would you assign percentages of humanity and divinity to Jesus? Could he be 50 percent human and 50 percent divine, so that he adds up to 100 percent Jesus? To say that, though, contradicts what we have said both in the last chapter and this chapter. He is "of one being with the Father," and thus 100 percent divine. And he is also "like us in every respect" and thus 100 percent human. So, is Jesus 200 percent, and how could that be possible? This is the tension and confusion that the heresies of Arius and the Docetists sought to lessen. But authentic faith is found in keeping the tension. The nature of Jesus's divinity and humanity isn't a math problem to solve but a faith solution to believe.

For Our Sake

It may be surprising to find that the Nicene Creed completely passes over the aspects of Jesus's earthly ministry that are usually the focus of Lent. There is no account of his baptism, temptation in the wilderness, calling of disciples, transfiguration, miracles, parables, or triumphant procession into Jerusalem on Palm Sunday. The reason for this is that these aspects of Jesus's life were not the subject of debate at the council. This is not to say they are unimportant, just that no one was arguing about them in Nicaea.

Instead, the creed goes directly from Christmas to Good Friday, from the Incarnation to the Crucifixion, from when Christ appeared in the flesh for our sake to when his flesh was pierced for our sake. And once again, this line in the creed includes a historical marker. Jesus was crucified *under Pontius Pilate*, an imperial official whose administration was recorded and is well attested in sources outside of the Gospels. (And for the record, Pilate's reputation in those sources is just as bad as it is in the Gospels.) Put another point in the column of Jesus's historical reality.

For Us and for Our Salvation

It is worth dwelling a moment on Pilate's inclusion in the creed. In the entire Nicene Creed, there are only two (non-divine) humans mentioned. They are Mary and Pilate. Mary caused Jesus's life to begin; Pilate caused it to end. Mary hears the angel's announcement and believes; Pilate hears Jesus himself and asks, "What is truth?" (John 18:38). Mary says, "Let it be with me according to your word" (Luke 1:38); Pilate washes his hands of it all. Mary is the archetype for faithfulness to God's plan; Pilate is the archetype for faithlessness. And yet, Pilate is used all the same, finding himself remembered forever for his role in our salvation.

The Crucifixion, which the creed considers here, is also described as "for our sake." This again reminds us that Jesus's life, death, and resurrection were undertaken for us. This was prophesied by Isaiah in a section of poetry termed the "Servant Songs." The fourth of those songs, Isaiah 53, says,

> *But he was wounded for our transgressions,*
> *   crushed for our iniquities;*
> *upon him was the punishment that made us whole,*
> *   and by his bruises we are healed.*
> *   (v. 5)*

Isaiah's lyrics connect Jesus's suffering to our salvation. Peter takes these verses from Isaiah and puts the matter more plainly. He writes, "He himself bore our sins in his body on the cross, so that, having died to sins, we might live for righteousness; by his wounds you have been healed" (1 Peter 2:24). And what was the problem for which we needed the Crucifixion? How was this accomplished?

This is what the creed gets at when it talks of Jesus being crucified "for our sake." There are many ways to interpret what Jesus accomplished on the cross. These are called "atonement theories," as they describe the way in which we are reconciled to God. Atonement theories answer the question, Exactly how does Jesus's death on the cross bring us redemption? A common atonement theory is penal substitutionary atonement, which holds that Jesus offered himself as a substitute to pay the price of our sins. Another is the *Christus victor*, or Christ-as-victor, theory. This understanding says that Jesus needed to die so that he could be raised victorious over the powers of sin and death. A third theory states that Jesus was needed as a ransom for sins, taking our place and allowing us to return to God. It's important to remember that the gospel is like a brilliant diamond and each theory of atonement examines this diamond from a different angle, appreciating the different beautiful facets of a singular reality. The point here is not to evaluate the validity of each atonement theory; the point is to show that Jesus's suffering and death on the cross was redemptive for us.

Taking Up His Cross

It is helpful to pause here on what we should and should not take away from Jesus's crucifixion. It is absolutely true that the pain and suffering endured by Jesus on the cross was the cause of our own healing and salvation. But we should be careful not to extrapolate too broadly the power of redemptive suffering. This is the belief that all suffering has redemptive purposes.

This kind of thinking is on display all around us. It's present anytime someone says something like, "God made me sick for a reason," "God wanted me to lose my job," or "God gave me this pain on purpose." While God can and does bring redemption and purpose out of suffering, that does not mean God is the cause of it or intended it. This idea is taken to the worst extreme when the Church refuses to help alleviate the suffering of others. If Christians believe that all suffering is redemptive, then we might hesitate to help prevent or lessen that suffering in others.

It's critical to remember, then, that Jesus is the only one who suffered and died for another's salvation. He did so as a human who was also fully God and with a sacrifice that was once-for-all. What he accomplished on the cross was effective and instructive in the proper light.

John Wesley, the founder of my denominational tradition, had a helpful way to see this in that proper light. Wesley distinguished between "bearing a cross" and "taking up your cross."[6] The former, Wesley said, refers to the suffering that we endure without a choice. This kind of suffering is not redemptive and is in no way necessary to our salvation. "Taking up your cross," on the other hand, means practicing self-denial, and it is indispensable to discipleship. This is what Jesus himself refers to in the several instances he instructs his disciples to "take up their cross" (see Matthew 10:38; 16:24; Mark 8:34; Luke 9:23; 14:27).

The Church's task, then, is to properly thread this needle. We ought to seek out anyone who is "bearing a cross" and help alleviate their suffering. At the same time, we ought to practice the self-denial found in "taking up our cross." And while doing both, we ought to give unending thanks to Christ for his redemptive, once-for-all sacrifice on the cross.

For the World

As a Methodist preacher, it is impossible for me to consider the sacrifice of Jesus on the cross without connecting it to Holy Communion. As pastors say when they place the piece of Communion bread in their congregants' hand, "This is the body of Christ, given for you." There is something about the mystery of Jesus's body represented in the bread that drives home the power and reality of what Jesus has done for us. At the Communion table, we truly "taste and see that the Lord is good" (Psalm 34:8).

I remember some years back bringing Communion to members of my church who were residents of a local long-term care facility. Onilee was one of those members. As I handed her a piece of bread small enough for her to manage, I said the usual blessing: "The body of Christ, given for you." At that, Onilee paused. She had received Communion countless times in her eighty-seven-year life. But in this moment, she held the bread up to her eyes. Gaze fixed on the bread, she repeated my words, her voice unsure: "The body of Christ, given...for me?" She was crying by the time I offered her the cup; I could tell that another level of the mystery had just opened to her. Onilee passed away the next week, and I know that she was welcomed into eternal rest by the same Savior whose presence she had just grasped in Communion.

There's something else incredible that happens in Communion. Not only do we receive the real presence of Christ in the bread and the cup, but through them, we become the body of Christ for the world. When the pastor invokes the blessing of the Holy Spirit on the Communion elements, a portion of the blessing goes like this: "Pour out your Holy Spirit on us gathered here, and on these gifts of bread and wine. Make them be for us the body and blood of Christ, that we may be for the world the body of Christ, redeemed by his blood."

> **Christ is present in Communion for us,**
> **so that we may present Christ to the world.**

Christ is present in Communion for us, so that we may present Christ to the world. Jesus was incarnate in the world for us and for our salvation, and we are called to continue that incarnating. We will return to this theme of the Church being the body of Christ in chapter 6. In the meantime, we find instructions for our life in Christ's incarnation and in the mystery of Holy Communion. Rather than withdraw from the world, we run into it with a sense of mission. Jesus did not keep his distance from the world, he "became flesh and blood, and moved into the neighborhood." So if we want to keep the promises we make in Communion, we should consider how we can move into our own neighborhoods in more real and effective ways.

Ministries that feed people, programs that provide a needed service, and mission activities that build relationships and fight isolation—these are all ways that we are "for the world the body of Christ." And it's all because Christ first gave his body for us and for our salvation.

Buried in the Grave

The creed dwells a moment longer on the events of Good Friday. The Council of Nicaea's participants were not content to say that Jesus was crucified; they elaborated that he "suffered death and was buried." This supplemental clause was added, like so much of the creed, for a specific purpose. There were some people, inside the Church and out, who did not believe that Jesus actually died on the cross. And if Jesus did not die on the cross, then his subsequent resurrection would be suspect, too.

This dates all the way back to the first Easter weekend. Matthew records that on the Saturday between Good Friday and Easter Sunday, the religious and political authorities colluded together. The Pharisees said to Pilate, "Command the tomb to be made secure until the third day; otherwise, his disciples may go and steal him away and tell the people, 'He has been raised from the dead'" (Matthew 27:64). Then, after the soldiers and stone guarding the tomb proved laughably ineffective at containing Jesus, the collusion resumed:

> *After the priests had assembled with the elders, they devised a plan to give a large sum of money to the soldiers, telling them, "You must say, 'His disciples came by night and stole him away while we were asleep.'*

If this comes to the governor's ears, we will satisfy him and keep you out of trouble." So they took the money and did as they were directed. And this story is still told among the Judeans to this day.

(Matthew 28:12-15)

Those religious and political authorities would rather pay to have uncomfortable truths go away than be confronted by them. The same is true of comfortable and powerful people today. And this is true even within the Church. Before and after the Council of Nicaea, there was a festering belief that Jesus did not actually die on the cross. Rather, they insisted, he was rescued at the last minute by God.

So, to push back firmly against this, the creed is clear that Jesus died and was buried. This is consistent with not only the Gospel accounts but also the earliest witness of the Church. In John's Gospel, when the Roman soldiers came forward to break Jesus's legs to speed along his crucifixion, they instead "saw that he was already dead" (19:33). Paul is emphatic at several points in his letters about the reality of Jesus's death. For Paul, it is a foundation of his understanding of salvation. "For while we were still weak, at the right time Christ died for the ungodly," Paul writes in Romans 5:6. A few sentences later, he writes, "But God proves his love for us in that while we still were sinners Christ died for us" (v. 8). To the church in Corinth, Paul summarizes the essential truth of the gospel this way: "that Christ died for our sins in accordance with the scriptures and that he was buried" (1 Corinthians 15:3-4).

Peter, finally, makes this point repeatedly. In three successive sermons—in Acts 2, 3, and 4—he includes the reality of Jesus's crucifixion and death. And in his first letter, he writes, "For Christ also suffered for sins once for all, the righteous for the unrighteous, in order to bring you to God" (1 Peter 3:18). Bringing things full circle for our chapter, Peter once again connects the reality of Jesus's crucifixion with our salvation. Jesus's death wasn't an accident. There was an "in order to" attached to it. It was, as the creed puts it, "for us and for our salvation."

For Real

As with the other sections of the Nicene Creed, what we claim about Jesus's humanity makes an enormous difference for our salvation and for our lives after receiving that salvation. In the last chapter, we discussed how Jesus's divinity was crucial because if Jesus is fully divine, then we are fully saved. The flip side of this is true, too. Jesus's humanity means that our salvation is for real. Otherwise, we're left with someone who is only like God becoming seemingly human. But that only leaves us with something like salvation and with a seeming presence of God. Instead, our Nicene faith is this: the real God became really human so that we could enjoy real salvation and real presence with God. Really!

This is a truth that the author of Hebrews marvels at. "For we do not have a high priest who is unable to sympathize with our weaknesses, but we have one who in every respect has been tested as we are, yet without sin. Let us therefore approach the throne of grace with boldness, so that we may receive mercy and find grace to help in time of need" (4:15-16). Jesus, whom Hebrews refers to as our high priest, was just like us in every way. Therefore, because of that truth, we can approach God's throne for mercy and grace. And not just approach it but approach it boldly! All because Jesus became human and purchased our salvation on the cross.

> **We know that the Crucifixion was not the end of the story.**

Of course, we know that the Crucifixion was not the end of the story. So let us now continue following the creed to see what it has to say about the resurrection, ascension, and second coming of Christ.

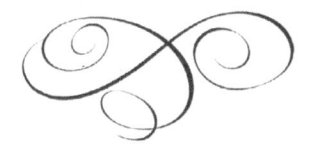

CHAPTER 4

In Accordance with the Scriptures

On the third day he rose again
in accordance with the Scriptures;
he ascended into heaven
and is seated at the right hand of the Father.
He will come again in glory
to judge the living and the dead,
and his kingdom will have no end.

A Predicted Surprise

On the first Easter Sunday, two men were making a joyless journey from Jerusalem to Emmaus, a small village about seven miles away. We don't know much about who these two were; we know only one of their names! But we know that they were depressed because of what had happened over the past few days. Their teacher, whom they called a prophet, had been crucified by the Romans and the chief priests. They had hoped, they confessed, that he would be Israel's redeemer. A foolish hope; no one takes on Rome and wins. The cross always has the final word.

Sure, some of the women in this prophet's group had surprised them that morning by reporting that their prophet's tomb was empty. They had even seen angels who reported that he was actually alive! But alas, he wasn't anywhere to be found. It seems like this might just be grief playing tricks on them. The cross, after all, always has the final word.

This scene is portrayed in the final chapter of Luke's Gospel. While these two disciples were walking and wallowing on their way to Emmaus, a mysterious visitor joins them. Luke tells us from the start that it is the risen Jesus but says that the disciples "were kept from recognizing him" (24:16). The cross, it seems, did not have the final word this time. This incognito Jesus feigns ignorance about his own crucifixion and resurrection (don't let anyone tell you God doesn't have a sense of humor!). After the disciples recount it all to him, Jesus lets his charade slip a little. Luke records it this way: "Then he said to them, 'Oh, how foolish you are and how slow of heart to believe all that the prophets have declared! Was it not necessary that the Messiah should suffer these things and then enter into his glory?' Then beginning with Moses and all the prophets, he interpreted to them the things about himself in all the scriptures" (vv. 25-27).

The disciples went on to Emmaus, where they shared a meal with the risen Jesus. As soon as Jesus broke bread, the disciples' eyes were opened. They exclaimed to each other, "Were not our hearts burning within us while he was talking to us on the road, while he was opening the scriptures to us?" (v. 32).

The Resurrection was a surprise for these disciples, as indeed it seemed to be for everyone who encountered the risen Jesus in the Gospel accounts. But, as Jesus said, it really should not have been a

In Accordance with the Scriptures

surprise. The Old Testament, Jesus unveiled for them, had plenty of clues. His resurrection was done "in accordance with the Scriptures," as the Nicene Creed says. This chapter traces how these final three acts of Jesus described in the creed—his resurrection, ascension, and second coming—were done to fulfill what had been spoken through the Prophets. Just as Jesus's birth and death were undertaken "for us and for our salvation," so his triumphant resurrection and return are accomplished according to the divine plan. A plan, Christians understand it, that had been plotted since the very earliest days of Israel's story.

> **The Resurrection was a surprise for these disciples, as indeed it seemed to be for everyone who encountered the risen Jesus in the Gospel accounts.**

Easter Eggs

I consider myself a bit of a movie and video game buff. And for eagle-eyed viewers and players, there is a feature to spot in many movies, shows, and games called *Easter eggs*. The term traces back to the video game *Adventure,* released by Atari in 1980. Atari had a policy of not crediting their game developers in the games, but *Adventure*'s developer, Warren Robinett, had a clever idea to get around this. If a player found a secret room in the game, they would see the message "Created by Warren Robinett." This wasn't caught until after the game was released, so Atari tried to put a positive spin on it, saying hidden things like this were "like Easter eggs for players to find."

Easter eggs have been put in games and movies ever since. For instance, in George Lucas's *Indiana Jones and the Raiders of the Lost Ark,* one scene finds Indiana Jones in a room covered with

61

We Believe

hieroglyphics. Blink and you'll miss one hieroglyph depicting R2-D2 and C-3PO, two characters from Lucas's other famous franchise, *Star Wars*. Similarly, the animation studio Pixar includes an Easter egg of its next project in each movie. In the 2001 movie *Monsters Inc.*, one character hands another a stuffed animal of an orange clownfish, hinting at the 2003 release of *Finding Nemo*. Then, in *Finding Nemo*, a character is seen reading a comic book of superhero Mr. Incredible, teeing up 2004's *The Incredibles*. And fans of Marvel superhero movies know that those films are packed to the gills with Easter eggs that are callbacks to old movies, hints about future movies, and obscure comic book references known only to the most die-hard fans.

    The great thing about Easter eggs is that they are not obvious the first time you see them. You only get *Finding Nemo*'s reference to *The Incredibles* once you've seen *The Incredibles* for yourself. And some Easter eggs are so brief or so hidden that it takes several viewings to realize you're seeing one. This is a great tactic for movie studios to drive ticket sales and streaming numbers. But it's also a way that Christians approach certain parts of the Old Testament.

    What Jesus told the disciples on the road to Emmaus was that the Old Testament contained several Easter eggs. What were these Easter eggs about? Well... Easter! And like Easter eggs in movies, shows, and games, these had been completely missed by the disciples. Only in light of the Resurrection do those Easter eggs become clear for what they are. Like Pixar carefully planning their movie projects and giving hints along the way, Christians read in the Old Testament a foretelling of the incarnation, crucifixion, and resurrection of his Son. Some of these Easter eggs had to do with the Resurrection itself, or about the three days spanning Good Friday and Easter Sunday, or about his second coming. All of these Easter eggs were placed so that Jesus's life could be shown to be "in accordance with the Scriptures," as the Nicene Creed says.

A Long Time Coming

The first book of the Bible, Genesis, records what many consider to be the first allusion to Jesus's resurrection on the third day. Genesis 22 opens with Abraham, the man whom God chose to become the father of his great nation, receiving a troubling command. God approaches Abraham and commands him to take his only son and sacrifice him. Sound familiar? Christians for millennia have seen parallels between what God tests Abraham to do with what God himself actually does in Jesus. Now, I should tell you that Abraham (and his son, Isaac) are ultimately spared from this terrible fate, further highlighting that God went to lengths no one else could in Jesus's sacrifice.

But what about the allusion to Jesus's resurrection? As Genesis 22 unfolds, Abraham dutifully saddles his donkey, grabs his firewood, and sets off with Isaac toward the mountain where the sacrifice is to take place. Verse 4 says, "On the third day Abraham looked up and saw the place far away." That is, when Abraham was prepared to sacrifice Isaac on the third day, he instead saw his life restored.

If that allusion sounds a little shaky, the author of Hebrews doesn't see it that way. In Hebrews 11 is a section often called the Hall of Faith, which notes the great faithful deeds of Old Testament heroes. Verse 17 in that chapter says, "By faith Abraham, when put to the test, offered up Isaac." Verse 19 continues, "He considered the fact that God is able even to raise someone from the dead—and figuratively speaking, he did receive him back." To the author of Hebrews, then, the scene with Abraham and Isaac is a type of resurrection, taking place on the third day.

There are other Scriptures that build out the foreshadowing of the Resurrection even more clearly. Hosea offers a call to repentance for the people of Israel, who he says have been "struck down." However, "on the third day he will raise us up" (6:1-2). When you consider that Jesus is the fulfillment of Israel and suffered death on our behalf, Hosea's words can be seen as referring to Jesus. Psalm 16:10 says, "For you did not give me up to Sheol [the underworld] / or let your faithful one see the Pit." While this psalm is ascribed to David, Peter had no qualms with asserting in Acts 2:31 that David actually "spoke of the resurrection of the Messiah."

The clearest foreshadowing of Jesus's resurrection on the third day was pointed out by Jesus himself beforehand. In Matthew's Gospel, Jesus was told by some religious leaders, "Teacher, we wish to see a sign from you" (12:38). Apparently fed up with them, Jesus responded, "An evil and adulterous generation asks for a sign, but no sign will be given to it except the sign of the prophet Jonah" (v. 39).

Reach back to your vacation Bible school days and remember the story of Jonah. Jonah was a prophet sent to call the wicked city of Nineveh to repentance. Instead of trekking to Nineveh, however, Jonah cuts a path in the opposite direction, even taking passage on a ship in the Mediterranean Sea. But a storm whips up, and Jonah ends up being tossed overboard, where he spends three days and three nights in the belly of a large fish. Jesus makes the connection clear: "For just as Jonah was three days and three nights in the belly of the sea monster, so for three days and three nights the Son of Man will be in the heart of the earth" (Matthew 12:40).

It is for these reasons that Paul can confidently assert in 1 Corinthians 15, "Christ died for our sins in accordance with the scriptures...he was buried and...he was raised on the third day in accordance with the scriptures" (vv. 3-4). It is that repetition of "in accordance with the scriptures" that the Council of Nicaea borrowed for this portion of the creed. But the Resurrection was not the only event that Nicaea pulled from Scripture.

The Ascension

Forty days after being raised from death, Jesus was raised once again. Paul put it eloquently to the Ephesians: "He who descended is the same one who ascended far above all the heavens, so that he might fill all things" (Ephesians 4:10). In this way, Jesus completed his round-trip journey. Beginning in heaven as the eternally begotten Word of God, Jesus descended to earth in the Incarnation. Between the Crucifixion and the Resurrection, he descended further still, so that no place would be outside of his experience and presence. Then he begins his ascension on Easter Sunday, providing witness and encouragement to his disciples. Finally, he ascends further still to heaven, fulfilling what David sang in Psalm 139,

> *Where can I go from your spirit?*
> *Or where can I flee from your presence?*
> *If I ascend to heaven, you are there;*
> *if I make my bed in Sheol, you are there.*
> *(vv. 7-8)*

The Ascension is recorded or referenced in three of the Gospels and in the Book of Acts. Matthew ends his Gospel with an ascension of sorts. In that scene, Jesus commissions his disciples, saying, "Go therefore and make disciples of all nations" (28:19). John's Gospel doesn't record the Ascension outright, but the risen Jesus does reference it to Mary Magdalene outside the tomb on Easter morning. When she runs to embrace him, he stops her, saying, "Do not touch me, because I have not yet ascended to the Father" (20:17).

It is Luke, then, who gives us the clearest account of the Ascension. In the closing verses of his Gospel, after the Emmaus story that opened this chapter, Luke describes how Jesus ascended: "Then he led them out as far as Bethany, and, lifting up his hands, he blessed them. While he was blessing them, he withdrew from them and was carried up into heaven" (Luke 24:50-51). This account is given fuller detail in the opening chapter of Luke's sequel, the Book of Acts. Jesus speaks this blessing over the apostles: "But you will receive power when the Holy Spirit has come upon you, and you will be my witnesses in Jerusalem, in all Judea and Samaria, and to the ends of the earth" (Acts 1:8). And with that, "as they were watching, he was lifted up, and a cloud took him out of their sight" (1:9).

What follows is a humorous scene. Having just witnessed their risen Lord rise again into the clouds, the apostles are understandably overawed. I like to think it probably looked like it did when I used to take my oldest child to watch airplanes. When he was a toddler, we would go to the small airport near our house, and he would watch the small four-seater Cessna airplanes taxi and take off. On a clear day, he would follow the skyward plane for miles, until it was no more than a speck against a blue sky. But he was transfixed, so much so that someone who walked up just then might ask what the angels asked the apostles: "Why do you stand looking up toward heaven?" (Acts 1:11).

> **The empowering presence of the promised Holy Spirit enlivens the Church for the mission that takes up the rest of the New Testament.**

These heavenly disrupters snap the apostles out of their stupor, saying, "This Jesus, who has been taken up from you into heaven, will come in the same way as you saw him go into heaven." All of church history takes place between the beginning and end of that sentence. That is, Jesus will come again; but in the meantime, we have work to do! The empowering presence of the promised Holy Spirit enlivens the Church for the mission that takes up the rest of the New Testament. It continues to this day, and it will continue until Christ returns.

In Accordance with the Scriptures

Just as the creed moves from Jesus's ascension to his second coming, so do these angels remind the apostles that Christ will be returning one day. But before the creed gets to that glorious day, it first tells us where Christ is while we wait and work.

Right-Hand Man

I am left-handed, and I'm a little bitter about it. Sure, 18 percent of US presidents have been left-handed, despite left-handers composing only 10 percent of the general population. And yes, southpaws are better first basemen than their right-handed baseball teammates. It's likely, science suggests, that left-handed people are naturally more creative and imaginative. But lefties like me need all the benefits we can get to overcome a steep disadvantage.

Historically, the right side has been favored. It's no accident that the English word *right* can mean both "correct" and "the opposite of left." In Latin, the word for "left" is *sinister*! And in the Greek of the New Testament, the word for "left" can also mean "stupid."[1] This stretches back to the Bible. In the time of the patriarchs of Genesis, a blessing given by the right hand was greater than one given by the left hand (Genesis 48:8-22). The Teacher in Ecclesiastes puts it more bluntly: "The heart of the wise inclines to the right, / but the heart of a fool to the left" (Ecclesiastes 10:2). Jesus even gets in on this, foretelling of a time when he separates the righteous from the unrighteous (Matthew 25:31-46). As you might expect by now, the righteous go to his right side, and the unrighteous his left.

It should come as no surprise, then, that when Jesus ascends into heaven, he goes to "the right hand of the Father," as the creed asserts. This, too, is scriptural. It comes most clearly from Psalm 110, which is the New Testament's most quoted psalm. The psalm, attributed to David, begins with, "The LORD says to my lord, / 'Sit at my right hand

67

/ until I make your enemies your footstool.'" This one verse contains a rich vein of truth. Not only do we have the designation of Jesus sitting at the Father's right hand but we also have a word about who Jesus is. Jesus uses this verse in his arguments with the religious leaders of his day, noting that this verse has David, the great king of Israel, referring to someone in addition to the Lord as his "lord." Who could this lord be? None other than the one Lord, Jesus Christ.

The opening verses of Hebrews reinforce this placement of Jesus at the right hand of the Father. In an earlier chapter, we included Hebrews 1:3, with its insistence that Jesus is of one substance with the Father. "He is the reflection of God's glory and the exact imprint of God's very being." The second half of that verse then details Jesus's return to his Father's side: "When he had made purification for sins, he sat down at the right hand of the Majesty on high."

At his Father's side, Jesus is now in a position to intercede on our behalf and prepare a place for us. This is what he promised his disciples in John 14: "In my Father's house there are many dwelling places. If it were not so, would I have told you that I go to prepare a place for you? And if I go and prepare a place for you, I will come again and will take you to myself, so that where I am, there you may be also" (vv. 2-3). And while we wait, we have a very important job to do.

Good Stewards

J. R. R. Tolkien's *The Lord of the Rings* contains many themes from Scripture that relate to Tolkien's deep Christian faith. One of those allegories comes in the character of Denethor, Steward of Gondor. Gondor is a kingdom that has been without a king for almost a thousand years; in the king's stead is the steward, who administers the kingdom under the king's authority. Over the centuries, the idea that Gondor's king would return grew dimmer and dimmer, until the stewards thought of themselves as kings in all but name.

In Accordance with the Scriptures

When the protagonists of Tolkien's saga meet Denethor, he expresses this sentiment, saying, "The rule of Gondor...is mine and no other man's, unless the king should come again."[2] The phrase "unless the king should come again" comes almost as an afterthought. Because, as the events of the story make clear, Denethor considers himself Gondor's rightful ruler.

We are in a similar situation today. Our King has gone, vanished from our sight, but he will return one day. In the meantime, we are not rulers in our own authority, no matter our political or military titles. Instead, we are stewards. This was our original task, given back in Genesis 1. God tells our oldest ancestors, "Be fruitful and multiply and fill the earth and subdue it and have dominion" (v. 28). We are stewards, given the task of shepherding God's creation under our Lord's authority. This is continued in Matthew 28 in the so-called Great Commission, when Jesus tells the disciples, "All authority in heaven and on earth has been given to me. Go therefore and make disciples of all nations" (vv. 18-19). Jesus has all authority, and he has deputized us as his stewards while we await his return. This is what we mean in the church by "stewardship."

When many of us hear the word *stewardship*, we think of giving financially to the church and of annual stewardship campaigns. And while financial stewardship is a crucial part of stewardship, the full picture includes much more. Everything that we do (and don't do) has a bearing on our stewardship. Because we are stewards, trusted agents of our King, everything we do is a reflection of his reign. How we spend our time and resources tells others about our King's priorities. How we interact with friends and enemies gives color to what citizenship is like in his kingdom. Even how we engage politically has implications on that kingdom's agenda.

While we await our King's return, it can be hard to remember that this return will come one day. Like Denethor, we would do well to consider how we can be better and more faithful stewards. For Denethor, the jig was up when one of *The Lord of the Rings*'s heroes, Aragorn, turns out to be Gondor's long-lost king. And just like Aragorn, our King will return one day. It is that return, promised by Jesus, to which the creed, and we, now turn.

The Second Coming

A visit from a world leader or dignitary is a big deal. A president passing through a town will draw a huge crowd, and a queen's tour of overseas territory is an occasion for celebration. This was true to an even greater extent in the ancient world, before jets could ferry important people across the globe in a day. Cities visited by a king or emperor would remember and celebrate the event for centuries. The Greeks even had a word for a visit like this: a *parousia*. Eagle-eyed readers will spot in that word the *ousia* we discussed in chapter 2 on the Son's identical *ousia*, or "being," with the Father. The prefix *para* means "beside"; hence a paraprofessional in a classroom works beside the class's teacher. *Parousia*, then, means "being beside," like when a king comes to town to be among its people.

Parousia is the technical term used to describe Jesus's second coming. Like so many of Jesus's parables, the action turns on the *parousia*, or return, of the parable's authority figure. It is the nobleman who returns after entrusting servants with vast sums of money (Luke 19:11-27; Matthew 25:14-30); the groom who arrives belatedly to the wedding banquet, catching some bridesmaids by surprise (Matthew 25:1-13); the owner of the vineyard who comes to evict wicked tenants (Matthew 21:33-46); and the master who returns unexpectedly (Matthew 24:45-51). Over and over again, Christ's *parousia* is the great event that ushers in a new and different age.

Two letters in the New Testament are chiefly concerned with the *Parousia*: 2 Thessalonians and 2 Peter. Like Christians ever since, the recipients of these two letters are anxious about the particulars. *When* will it happen? *What* will it be like? *Who* should we listen to about it? Paul and Peter's words are intended to calm nerves and rebuke false teachers. "As to the coming of our Lord Jesus Christ..., we beg you, brothers and sisters, not to be quickly shaken in mind or alarmed" (2 Thessalonians 2:1-2). We would do well to remember these words the next time some flashy preacher tells us he knows the *when, what,* and *how* of the Second Coming. Even the Son doesn't know when he's coming back (Matthew 24:36)! For all we know, Jesus will come back before you finish this sentence.

In the Old Testament, this gravely important event is referred to as the "Day of the Lord," and it is explained by the Prophets as a day of judgment and divine presence. Like the *Parousia*, it refers to the time when God will visit the earth and all will be made right. This is variously good news for some and bad news for others, depending on where one shakes out in that judgment. As it turns out, the creed discusses a bit of the judgment that the *Parousia* promises.

A Judgment Call

The idea of a divine judgment can be a touchy subject in some circles these days. Many of us don't like to hear about judgment. We remind one another that Jesus said, "Judge not, that ye be not judged. / For with what judgment ye judge, ye shall be judged" (Matthew 7:1-2a KJV), as if that was all he said on the subject (it wasn't). We chide one another for perceived judginess. A while back, I even had a membership at a gym that boasted about being a "judgement free zone."

Divine judgment, however, is not only an unavoidable truth in Scripture; it is also an act of Christ's good grace. First, let's look at the scriptural warrant. The creed's declaration that Christ will "judge the living and the dead" is lifted straight from Paul's second letter to Timothy. In the final chapter of the letter that Paul wrote to his young protégé, he begins his closing charge to faithfulness by saying, "In the presence of God and of Christ Jesus, who is to judge the living and the dead" (2 Timothy 4:1). In John's Revelation, before describing the "new heaven and the new earth" that await us, he first sees that "all were judged according to what they had done" (Revelation 20:13). Even in the Old Testament, Daniel records an awesome scene where Jesus, referred to here as the "Ancient of Days," holds judgment in a heavenly court (Daniel 7).

But in a world that values self-determination and rejects ultimate claims of truth, is believing in something like the Last Judgment outdated and cruel? Is imagining a scene in which Christ separates sheep from goats (Matthew 25:32-33) not an exercise in vengefulness? The Council of Nicaea didn't think so, and neither did the biblical prophets. Sticking with the imagery of sheep and goats, the prophet Ezekiel foretold of a time when the Good Shepherd of Israel would search, sort, and judge between his sheep.

Why? Because some sheep have "pushed with flank and shoulder and butted at all the weak animals with your horns until you scattered them far and wide" (Ezekiel 34:21). Ezekiel is speaking metaphorically of all the ways we have used and abused others, a problem no less common now than it was then. The Good Shepherd judging between and separating his flock isn't cruel; it would be cruel not to.

> **Only God is able to strike this delicate balancing act between justice and mercy, because only God is the Creator of both justice and mercy.**

Our judge is not only just and righteous but also "gracious and merciful, / slow to anger, abounding in steadfast love, / and relenting from punishment" (Joel 2:13). Only God is able to strike this delicate balancing act between justice and mercy, because only God is the Creator of both justice and mercy. Whatever the parameters and characteristics of this judgment will be, however, one thing is clear. As author Fleming Rutledge writes, "The overall testimony of the Old and New Testaments is that God will save us *from* the judgment, but he will not save us *without* judgment."[3]

This is the grace of the Final Judgment. Speaking of this judgment on the Day of the Lord, the prophet Malachi says, "But who can endure the day of his coming, and who can stand when he appears? For he is like a refiner's fire and like washers' soap" (Malachi 3:2). Christ will "refine them like gold and silver, until they present offerings to the LORD in righteousness" (Malachi 3:3). This judgment will be a final act of grace, removing from us the sin that has clung to us so closely and so stubbornly, so that we are fit for God's redeemed creation.

We should not fear Christ's coming and judgment, then, but should welcome it. As John prays in the final words of Revelation, "Amen. Come, Lord Jesus" (Revelation 22:20). Come, we pray, and establish your unending kingdom.

According to Plan

There is something hopeful and delightful knowing that all of this was done according to God's plan, "in accordance with the Scriptures." We began this chapter in the uncertainty immediately before the Resurrection and ended it with Jesus's eternal and victorious reign.

Sometimes I wonder if the forces of sin and death were celebrating on that Saturday between the Crucifixion and the Resurrection. They had done it, they thought. They had taken care of God's latest

We Believe

attempt to free us from their clutches. They had killed the very Son of God, no less! It must have looked like a total victory on their part.

But this had always been God's plan. As we've seen, it had been set out from the first pages of Scripture. Death's victory was short-lived and as hollow as the empty grave was. This is why Paul's tone is so mocking: "Where, O death, is your victory? Where, O death, is your sting?" (1 Corinthians 15:55). What death had considered its ultimate victory was actually its ultimate defeat.

> **Our salvation always goes according to God's plan.**

Because this was always God's plan. There are bumps and detours along this plan; Scripture is full of these detours (Israel's forty-year wandering in the desert comes to mind). But the destination is never in doubt. And the same is true for our lives. Your life, like mine, is probably full of ups and downs. It has seasons of great faithfulness and moments of destructive sin. But for those of us who cling to the hope communicated in Scripture, we know that we can never be more than one prayer from God's side. This is the sense of Paul's great promise: "We know that all things work together for good for those who love God" (Romans 8:28). Hardship can and does come our way, but our salvation is secured. Because our salvation always goes according to God's plan. That plan finds its fulfillment in the creed's final line about Christ.

An Endless Hallelujah

When the angel Gabriel announced to Mary that she would bear the Son of God, he added to the promise traditionally given to the people of Israel. Back in 2 Samuel 7, God promised King David, "Your house and your kingdom shall be made sure forever before me; your throne shall be established forever" (v. 16). This is the promise

In Accordance with the Scriptures

Gabriel speaks to Mary, then adds to it: "and of his kingdom there will be no end" (Luke 1:33). This is where the Nicene Creed borrows its final word about Christ, and it is a fitting place to end our chapter. The bulk of the creed, twenty-one of the thirty-five lines, deals with God the Son. Like the rest of the creed, there has not been a line about Jesus without some basis in Scripture. This chapter has traced how the resurrection, ascension, and *parousia* of Jesus are not only found in Scripture but are also fulfillments of some of Scripture's deepest promises. This is most plainly and beautifully seen in the fulfillment of Christ's eternal kingdom.

The grand arc of Scripture has been one of redemption. From Genesis 3 on, Scripture is a rescue story, a millennia-spanning saga of a loving God heaven-bent on reuniting with his creation. The Incarnation was a covert operation, a special ops mission with God the Son going behind enemy lines to break us out of death's grip from the inside. The Crucifixion was, as N. T. Wright put it, "the day the revolution began."[4] Pentecost was the establishment and empowerment of forward bases and outposts. The Second Coming, the *Parousia*, though, is when the forces of sin and death are decisively dealt with. At last, at long last, Christ's kingdom will come, and the long-standing promises of Scripture will be fulfilled. What's old will be new again: a river of life will flow from God's perfect garden (Genesis 2:10; Revelation 22:1). A tree of life will welcome us all in its shade (Genesis 2:9; Revelation 22:2). God himself will dwell with us (Genesis 3:8; Revelation 22:3).

Genesis and Revelation, the first and the last books of the Bible, the alpha and the omega, contain parallel promises of what Christ's kingdom will bring. "In accordance with the Scriptures," indeed.

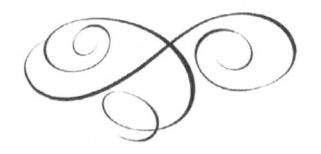

CHAPTER 5

With the Father and the Son

We believe in the Holy Spirit, the Lord, the giver of life,
who proceeds from the Father and the Son,
who with the Father and the Son
is worshiped and glorified,
who has spoken through the prophets.

The Forgotten God

The Council of Nicaea largely dealt with the swirling controversies surrounding the relationship between God the Father and God the Son. Because of this, less attention was given to God the Spirit, who must share space in the third and final section of the Nicene Creed with words about the Church. As we discussed in chapter 1, however, the already-existing creeds pre-Nicaea had developed the threefold format of Father, Son, and Holy Spirit to match the words used in baptismal vows. So, in beginning the closing section of their creed, the participants of the Council of Nicaea turned to the Holy Spirit.

Because of the brief treatment, however, the Holy Spirit tends to be minimized in the eyes and hearts of some Christians. To a degree, it's understandable. God the Father is present and active throughout the Old Testament—walking in the garden of Eden with Adam and Eve, conversing with Abraham, giving the Law to Moses, to name just a few examples. God the Son is also easy to conceptualize. Jesus walked on earth with us and spoke words that we can still read in the Gospels. But God the Spirit? Especially in our culture today, the language of a "Holy Spirit" is a little harder to grasp.

Let's look for a moment, then, at how the Holy Spirit has been described. This description comes from St. Basil the Great, who was born five years after the Council of Nicaea and lived in the pivotal years that cemented Nicaea's legacy:

> Everything that needs holiness turns to him. All that live virtuously desire him, as they are watered by his inspiration and assisted toward their proper and natural end. He perfects others, but himself lacks nothing. He lives, but not because he has been restored to life; rather, he is the source of life. He does not grow in strength gradually, but is complete all at once. He is established in himself and present everywhere. He is the source of holiness, an intellectual light for every rational power's discovery of truth, supplying clarity, so to say, through himself. He is inaccessible in nature, but approachable in goodness.[1]

Basil's words, as we'll see, draw from the words about the Holy Spirit in the Nicene Creed. Before we get more into that, however, we should pause for another moment on the trinitarian nature of God.

One in Three

As we discussed in chapter 2, the word *Trinity* is nowhere found in Scripture. Rather, the understanding of our God as "one God in three Persons" developed in the years after the events of the New

Testament. As Christians grappled with their faith, they deepened their understanding of God. This was, as it happens, thanks in part to the work of the Holy Spirit, who guides us to the truth (see John 16:12-14). And the Holy Spirit led them to understand that God is at once three Persons in one God.

The number three in the world of the Bible symbolizes completeness. Ecclesiastes 4:12 says, "And though one might prevail against another, two will withstand one. A threefold cord is not quickly broken." Oftentimes, things are repeated three times in Scripture to communicate emphasis and finality. God calls to Samuel three times; Jesus prays in the garden of Gethsemane three times; Peter denies Jesus three times and is reinstated by him after being asked "Do you love me?" three times. Three units of time account for a complete journey, whether it's Jonah in the belly of the fish for three days, or Jesus's own three days in the tomb.

Even outside the world of Scripture, three is considered special for its completeness. The ancient Greek mathematician Pythagoras considered three to be the perfect number, so much so that geometry students today are still using his Pythagorean theorem to determine the length of sides on triangles. There's a reason that we do something "on the count of three" when we want to synchronize an action, and there's a reason that we say that "the third time's the charm."

That reason is because of the Trinity. God's threefold nature, while not explicitly spelled out in Scripture, is self-evident in his creation. Everything leads to an understanding that our one God is indeed three Persons. Anything less than three just isn't complete. As Harry Nilsson sang (and Three Dog Night sang better), "One is the loneliest number" and does not capture the divine communion of our God. Two is a binary that too often represents division and difference (good vs. evil, heaven vs. hell, Republicans vs. Democrats). Three, however, draws everything into completeness.

We Believe

In that sense, the Council of Nicaea was able to move past some of their dilemmas surrounding the relationship between God the Father and God the Son by remembering God the Spirit. Instead of succumbing to some of the heresies we have discussed in previous chapters, which set the Son against the Father, the Spirit completes the picture of cooperation among the Persons of the Godhead.

Three in One

That term "Godhead" needs some unpacking. Simply put, "Godhead" means the things that are characteristic of God. The suffix "-head" is an old English term that has largely been replaced by "-hood" in most words today. We used to talk about important people being knighted into the "knighthead"; now we say "knighthood." We used to delineate masculine things as belonging to "manhead" and feminine things as belonging to "womanhead"; now we say manhood, womanhood, and personhood.[2] But because "Godhead" is a scriptural term, pious English speakers left it the old fashioned way.[3] For our purposes, then, it might be easier to speak of it as Godhood; that is, those things that are characteristic of God.

> **There are three Persons, but only one God. Father, Son, and Holy Spirit, in one God.**

The important thing to note here is that there is only one Godhead, or Godhood. There are three Persons, but only one God. Father, Son, and Holy Spirit, in one God. All three Persons enjoy all the characteristics of the Godhood, and it is incomplete to talk about the Godhood without one or more of these three Persons. For this reason, St. Athanasius, who was the bishop of Alexandria's assistant at the Council of Nicaea, would later write, "And the catholic [universal] faith is this: That we worship one God in Trinity, and Trinity in Unity."[4]

This understandably causes confusion. It is difficult to wrap our heads around the truth that we worship one God who is yet three Persons. There is a poignant story from church history that illustrates this. In the late 700s, a man named Timothy was the patriarch, or head, of the church in Baghdad. One day, Patriarch Timothy was called before the ruler of the Muslim empire that stretched from Egypt to India with its capital in Baghdad. The emperor, al-Mahdi, wanted answers from Timothy on what Christianity believed. He had heard about the Trinity, and it just didn't make sense to him.

He started the conversation, "If God is one, he is not three; and if he is three, he is not one; what is this contradiction?"[5] The Trinity was a math problem that al-Mahdi could not solve. And this was a man who liked math problems; his scholars at the university near his palace were busy inventing a new kind of math called *al-jabr* (we just call it algebra today). And just like middle schoolers today know, if x = 1, then x ≠ 3. So if God is one, how could God also be three?

Al-Mahdi's problem, Patriarch Timothy tells him, is that the Trinity isn't a math problem but a faith solution. Pressed for an explanation or analogy to satisfy this algebra problem, Timothy finally says, "There is no other God like him, from whom I might draw a demonstration."[6] The triune nature of God is not something we must understand before we can believe it. Rather, we believe it first, and then we experience it. In this way, understanding the Trinity is like understanding the Holy Spirit, who is the Third Person of the Trinity. We might not be able to experience the Holy Spirit with our senses of sight, touch, taste, hearing, or smell, but we don't need to. The proof is not something we have to work out ourselves, but rather receive as a gift.

With some trinitarian foundation established, we can turn to how the Nicene Creed describes this Third Person of the Trinity.

Life-Giver

In Romans 8, the apostle Paul gets to the climax of his letter. Coming at the midpoint of his sixteen-chapter magnum opus, Romans 8 is a tour de force in praise of the Holy Spirit and its power in our lives. Because Christ has dealt decisively with sin and death, we can now "live according to the Spirit" (v. 5). What does this mean? It means that "the Spirit of God dwells in you" (v. 9). With that, Paul begins to hit his stride: "If the Spirit of him who raised Jesus from the dead dwells in you, he who raised Christ Jesus from the dead will give life to your mortal bodies also through his Spirit that dwells in you" (v. 11).

Did you catch the Trinity in that verse? It is the Holy Spirit of God the Father who raised God the Son from the dead. That same Spirit, Paul says, will also "give life" to us. It is this term that the Nicene Creed borrows when it terms the Holy Spirit "the giver of life." As Basil said at the beginning of this chapter, the Spirit is the "source of life."

The Spirit has been involved in giving life from the very beginning. The word for "spirit" in both the Hebrew and Greek of the Bible points to an incredible truth. In Hebrew, the word is *ruach*, and in Greek it's *pneuma*. What's incredible is that both *ruach* and *pneuma* mean not only "spirit" but also "wind" and "breath." So in Genesis 2, when God creates the first human, this is how it happens. "Then the LORD God formed man from the dust of the ground and breathed into his nostrils the breath of life, and the man became a living being" (v. 7). It was the Spirit, the life-giver, whom God breathed into us to give us life.

With the Father and the Son

In Ezekiel 37, God leads the prophet to a valley full of dry bones. To reinforce just how long these bones have been there, verse 2 tells us, "They were very dry." God asks an obvious question to Ezekiel: "Can these bones live?" (v. 3). Of course not! But God has planned a demonstration of just how powerful the Holy Spirit, the giver of life, really is. God commands Ezekiel to prophesy: "Thus says the Lord GOD to these bones: I will cause breath to enter you, and you shall live... and you shall know that I am the LORD" (vv. 5, 6).

In the same way, when the risen Jesus appears to his disciples, he gives the Holy Spirit to them by breathing. John 20:22 says, "He breathed on them and said to them, 'Receive the Holy Spirit.'" When the Holy Spirit is breathed or blown in, life follows—life that enlivens, invigorates, and inspires. Without the Holy Spirit, there is no life. Psalm 104 says of God and creation, "When you take away their breath [spirit], / they die and return to the dust" (v. 29). But conversely, "When you send for your spirit [breath], / they are created" (v. 30).

The Power of the Spirit

With the life breathed by the Spirit also comes power. This power is something that many people can testify to; it was promised in Scripture and has been experienced by many people throughout the Church's history. I count myself among that group. As I shared back on the first page of chapter 1, I have had a speech impediment my entire life. In middle school, my geometry teacher asked the school's guidance counselor if I was certifiably mute. I just refused to talk, lest my profound stutter cause stares or laughter. As an aside, I'll never forgive whoever decided to make the word *stutter* begin with an *st*: probably the same guy who put an *s* in *lisp*.

We Believe

> **With the life breathed by
> the Spirit also comes power.**

This stutter made it all the more confusing when, before my senior year of high school, I felt the Holy Spirit nudging me toward a career in ministry. I remember thinking, "Why would God want me to preach to others when I can't even say 'God'?" Like most people faced with a call to ministry, I pushed the thought to the back of my mind. But it kept coming back, louder and louder. One day after school, I couldn't take it anymore, so I drove to my church and walked into my youth pastor's office. I told Adam, my youth pastor, what I felt like the Holy Spirit had been telling me. In one of those moments that change a life's trajectory with a single sentence, Adam responded, "I'm glad you shared that with me, Michael; I've been meaning to tell you the same thing for a while now."

Before long, he had me preaching in front of the entire congregation of Ardmore First UMC. It was the day after my eighteenth birthday, and what was the chosen text that day? Acts 1:8: "You will receive power when the Holy Spirit has come upon you, and you will be my witnesses in Jerusalem, in all Judea and Samaria, and to the ends of the earth." Again, don't let anyone tell you that God doesn't have a sense of humor!

Since that first sermon, I have preached over 250 times. Every single time, it's not something I am doing in my own power. Were it up to me, I would be holed up somewhere in a nice cubicle or office, in the safety and comfort of my spreadsheets. But thanks be to God that it isn't up to me. And thanks be to God that there is Spirit-given power to match Spirit-given purpose. To be sure, a good speech therapist has also been very helpful. And I am still careful in making sure my sentences don't start with words or sounds that are difficult for me. And still, in addition to all that, every time I get up to proclaim God's love and power in a sermon, I say a little prayer. And that love and power haven't failed me yet.

Cause for Schism

The Holy Spirit is life-giving and powerful, but how does it get to us in order to give us this life and power? This is the question that the Nicene Creed next addresses, and it is around this section that a controversy cropped up centuries after the Council of Nicaea. Most denominations' versions of the Nicene Creed say that the Spirit "proceeds from the Father and the Son." The problem is that the original creed decided on at Nicaea did not have the phrase "and the Son." Christians in the Latin-speaking West inserted it into their recitation of the Nicene Creed in the years after Nicaea, while the Greek-speaking Eastern churches did not.

The addition of the words "and from the Son" became known as the *Filioque* controversy, as *Filioque* is how you would say "and from the Son" in Latin. Among other issues, the addition of the *Filioque* clause into the Nicene Creed was a cause of the so-called Great Schism between the Eastern and Western branches of Christianity in 1054. Ever since, the Western church (centered in Rome and called the Roman Catholic Church) has been separated from the Eastern churches, which are called Orthodox. From there, of course, several denominations have split from the Roman Catholic Church, so now the great family tree of the Church has many branches. This will come up again in the next chapter when we consider how the creed says that the Church is "one."

The Latin Christians had good reason to believe that the Holy Spirit proceeds from the Son as well as the Father. They referred to John 20, quoted above, when Jesus breathed on the disciples the Holy

Spirit. In a very literal sense, then, the Holy Spirit "proceeded" from Jesus. Earlier in John's Gospel, Jesus told his disciples that "I will send to you" the Holy Spirit (15:26).

On the other hand, the Eastern Orthodox Church would say, Jesus says in that same sentence that the Spirit "comes from the Father." And the Greek Christians had further reasons to resist the inclusion of the *Filioque* clause. Their concern was that having the Spirit proceed from both the Father and the Son would mean that there are two "sources" for the Spirit. That is, the *Filioque* clause implies that the Spirit originates in both the Father and the Son. But as the creed states at its beginning, God the Father is the maker of everything. Hence, he alone can be the source.

A possible middle ground actually predates Nicaea by one hundred years. A leader in the early Church named Tertullian, who lived in the early 200s, wrote that the "Spirit is *from* the Father *through* the Son."[7] That is, the Father is the source of the Holy Spirit and sends it to us through the Son. This is echoed by St. Basil, whom we met earlier, writing that the Spirit is "joined through the one Son to the one Father."[8]

At this point, it can be easy to get caught up in the prepositions flying everywhere. Is the Holy Spirit *through* or *to*? Is it *from* the Son or *through* him? It is especially confusing because this debate between two languages, Latin and Greek, is now being laundered through a third language, English, in this chapter. The preposition game, however, belies the real conflict between the Eastern and Western branches of Christianity. "The creed *without* the *Filioque* clause became a marker of the Eastern Orthodox identity, just as the creed *with* the *Filioque* clause became a marker of the Roman Catholic."[9] This led to disastrous division and heartache. "The two versions of the creed, with and without the *Filioque*, came to be deployed as weapons of identity politics" between the two branches.[10]

For our purposes here, we can acknowledge legitimate concerns on both sides. On the one side, the Filioque clause has merit as a faith claim. On the other hand, however, it was inserted into the Nicene Creed without the input and approval of the entire Church. What made the Council of Nicaea so impactful was that it gathered representatives from the entire Church into one decision-making body. The witness of Nicaea has been marred, somewhat, by one half of the worldwide Church reciting a line that was not originally included. Now, seventeen hundred years after the council, representatives of the Roman Catholic and Orthodox Churches are having conversations that may yet lead to a mutual understanding. For the unity of Christ's Church and the witness of the Nicene Creed, let us pray that reconciliation can be had.

Together, Together, Together

Let us leave behind the *Filioque* controversy and, with the creed, return to less controversial ground, at least in our time. The creed says that the Holy Spirit "with the Father and the Son is worshiped and glorified." As we've seen in other places, however, the English translation of the original Greek of the creed loses some pretty incredible features. A more accurate word-for-word translation of this clause would be "who together with the Father and the Son are worshiped together and glorified together." Three "togethers" in one sentence? You can see why English translators have opted to make it cleaner.

But there is a reason for this triple repetition. Like we discussed above with the Trinity, there is a power and purpose for repeating something three times: it communicates completeness. Having to slow down over the clunkiness of repeating "together" three times really drives home the point that Father, Son, and Spirit are worshiped and glorified together. While I don't think this clunky translation will catch on anytime soon, hopefully you'll be reminded of it each time you recite the creed.

The members of the Council of Nicaea had another reason for being so forceful on this "togetherness." In addition to the controversies swirling around Nicaea related to God the Son, there were others pertaining to God the Spirit. Specifically, there were those who did not believe that the Holy Spirit should be worshiped or considered on equal footing with the Father and the Son. In their minds, the Holy Spirit was more of a "servant," being sent this way and that fulfilling the will of the Father. They would prefer to put an asterisk in the Trinity, with a footnote indicating that the Spirit should really be counted as under the Father and the Son.

The council pushed back forcefully on this. Relying on Scripture, they insisted that the Holy Spirit is worshiped and glorified alongside the Father and the Son. They relied on passages like John 4:24, when Jesus says to the Samaritan woman at the well, "God is Spirit, and those who worship him must worship in spirit and truth." And they turned to Paul, who writes in 2 Corinthians 3 that "now the Lord is the Spirit" (v. 17) and says that our transformation "comes from the Lord, the Spirit" (v. 18). Reflecting on this line in the creed, St. Basil writes that the Spirit is obviously worthy of giving glory to. The Spirit has done so much "that glory is nothing other than the recounting of the wonders that belong to him."[11]

> **The only way to worship the Trinity
> is together, together, together.**

With this, then, the Nicene Creed arrives at a full trinitarian faith. The Trinity would be further elaborated in the generation after the Council of Nicaea with St. Athanasius and his Athanasian Creed. Even without that fuller statement, though, the Nicene Creed sufficiently asserts our faith in one God in three Persons. By repeating "together" three times in its insistence that the Spirit be worshiped and glorified with the Father and the Son, the Nicene Creed makes it clear. The only way to worship the Trinity is together, together, together.

Spoken...

The Nicene Creed finishes its treatment of the Holy Spirit by saying that the Spirit has "spoken through the prophets." This is yet another subtle way of reminding us that the Spirit, like the Son, has been active and involved with God the Father from the very beginning. This, like everything else, is based on Scripture. The first verse of the Letter to the Hebrews says that before God sent Jesus to us, his Spirit "spoke to our ancestors in many and various ways by the prophets."

In the Old Testament, it was said that God's Spirit rested on Moses. When Moses appointed seventy elders to help lighten the burden of leadership, Numbers 11 says, "Then the LORD came down in the cloud and spoke to him and took some of the spirit that was on him and put it on the seventy elders, and when the spirit rested upon them, they prophesied" (v. 25). The prophet Joel explicitly linked the gift of the Spirit to prophesying when the Spirit said through him, "Then afterward I will pour out my spirit on all flesh; your sons and your daughters shall prophesy" (Joel 2:28). You may recognize those verses from the story of Pentecost in Acts 2, when Peter quotes them after receiving the Holy Spirit himself.

Isaiah, another memorable Old Testament prophet quoted in the New Testament, summarizes how prophets perform their task: "The spirit of the Lord God is upon me because the Lord has anointed me" (Isaiah 61:1). Jesus quotes this line in his first sermon at Nazareth in Luke 4, showing that he was continuing and fulfilling the prophetic witness. Of course, the presence and speaking of the Holy Spirit did not stop with Jesus. At Pentecost, the Holy Spirit was given, and the faithful continued to speak in the Spirit's power. After Pentecost, Acts records Peter, Stephen, Paul, twelve Ephesian Christians, and even the entire Church as "being filled with the Holy Spirit" and speaking with boldness (Acts 4:8; 7:55; 13:9; 19:6; and 4:31, respectively).

...and Speaking?

A lingering question remains for us as we finish our discussion on the Holy Spirit and turn in the next chapter to the work of the Church. Is the work of the Holy Spirit finished? When I was in seminary, there was a church not far from campus that had a banner facing the street that read, "The Spirit is still speaking." The banner's rainbow background made it clear that the "speaking" they were referring to was the ongoing debate surrounding human sexuality. Certainly, this is one area in which controversy rages today about whether doctrines of the Church can change over time.

As we discussed in chapter 2, we know that the Holy Spirit continued to speak to the Church after the last book of the Bible was written. It was the Holy Spirit that filled the Council of Nicaea with its presence, resulting in the Nicene Creed. Jesus promised that the Spirit "will guide you into all the truth" (John 16:13). He also promised that the Father gives us the Spirit "to be with you forever" and that he "will not leave you orphaned" (John 14:16, 18). Of course the Spirit is still speaking! As long as there is someone confessing that Jesus is Lord, the Holy Spirit is still speaking (see 1 Corinthians 12:3). As long as there is breath in our lungs, the Holy Spirit, the life-giver, is speaking.

That speaking, though, will not lead us astray. Just as we believe that the Spirit inspired the compilers of the Bible's canon and the authors of the Nicene Creed, we believe that those matters are settled (*Filioque* controversy notwithstanding!). So while the Spirit continues to guide us in truth, clarifying and refining our understanding of God and ourselves, the Spirit will not cause us to depart from these foundations. And as we trust the Spirit to guide us into clearer truth, we can be grateful for the guardrails of the Nicene Creed. The Nicene Creed provides for us the unalterable essentials of what it means to be Christian.

Christians, then, are free to seek the Spirit's speaking on things that do not take us beyond those essentials. Most denominational traditions have developed their doctrine in some way over their lifespans. The Roman Catholic Church developed the doctrine of purgatory with an appeal to Scripture, and then Protestants subsequently rejected it using their own scriptural basis. Some Protestant denominations have developed their understanding of God's calling of church leaders to include women, and they used Scripture to justify it. Some Christians baptize only those old enough to profess faith for themselves, while others baptize infants, with each group defending their practice with Scripture.

This is the beauty of the Christian mosaic. None of these positions runs afoul of the essentials listed in the Nicene Creed, so we have liberty to argue about them. Each denomination and each Christian can hold valid opinions on which of these positions is correct (this author certainly does), but we can also recognize that those on the opposing side have not left the Christian faith as defined by the bounds of the Nicene Creed.

The Nicene Creed, then, can serve as a tool for Christian charity and dialogue. When debates get heated, as they often do, between and within denominations, we can recognize that the Nicene Creed still draws us together. The matters of doctrine that we debate are important, and we ought to seek the Spirit's guidance with our whole selves. And as we debate, we ought to remember that we are doing so from within our Nicene enclosure.

Following the Spirit

In addition to major issues that impact entire denominations like those we just discussed, the Holy Spirit also speaks to us as individuals and individual churches. It is this speaking that brings to life for us the impact the Nicene Creed can have on our faith. As we remember that the Nicene Creed asserts that the Holy Spirit is "the giver of life," we are led to follow the Spirit into those things that give life. This means following the Spirit in activities, ministries, and practices that give life to ourselves, our communities, and the world around us. It was this following of the Spirit that led a former church of mine a few years back to purchase and forgive $3.5 million in medical debt from our neighbors. Here's how we did it.

In 2022, my church was preparing for our 150th anniversary as a church, having been organized as a church in 1872 by settlers in the newly admitted state of Nebraska. So, like any good Methodist church, we put together a committee to plan for this sesquicentennial (the fancy word for a 150th anniversary). We were planning all of the typical elements of a church anniversary: a special alumni choir, a sermon from the district superintendent, a catered luncheon after worship, and a historical open house. At the open house, we even had the saddlebags used by our first circuit-riding horseback preacher!

But as we planned, members of our planning committee wanted to do something more. Our church had been part of our community for so long, we wanted our anniversary to impact the community as well. We felt the Spirit leading us toward the biblical idea of a jubilee year (see Leviticus 25), a time every fifty years when debts are forgiven and relationships restored. At 150 years old, our church was in its third jubilee year, so we started looking for ways to make an impact along those lines. Some pastor friends of mine had recently partnered with a nonprofit called RIP Medical Debt (now it's called Undue Medical Debt) that buys medical debt from people whose bills had been sent to collections. They buy the debt for pennies on the dollar and then just forgive it, writing to the debtors that they no longer owe a dime. At the time, RIP Medical Debt promised they could forgive at least one hundred times what our campaign raised.

We liked this idea of forgiving debts in our jubilee year for people in our community. So we set a goal of raising $15,000, which we could use to forgive at least $1,500,000 in our 150th year, and got the word out. We blew right past that goal. As we heard stories about people's lives being changed from having their debt forgiven, our church was energized. The campaign gave my church life, and it gave life to the recipients of the debt forgiveness, too. By the time our campaign ended, we had wiped out $3,526,733 in defaulted medical debt for 3,855 families in five states. Not bad for a church with a $200,000 annual budget!

This is what it means for the Holy Spirit to be "the giver of life." In God's economy, there is no scarcity, only abundance. I'll be honest: some people on our planning committee were scared to undertake such an ambitious endeavor. What if we fail to meet our goal? If people gave to this campaign, would they not give as much to the church? But with the Spirit's life and power given to us, there was no room for fear. Because we did meet our goal, the success of our campaign inspired our families to give more to the church's general budget. It even inspired people to give to the church for the first time!

So whether it is a person with a stutter called to preach, or an ambitious church campaign, or whatever else the Spirit is calling us to do, we can be sure that following the Spirit will never let us down.

CHAPTER 6

One, Holy, Catholic, and Apostolic

We believe in one holy catholic and apostolic church.
We acknowledge one baptism
for the forgiveness of sins.
We look for the resurrection of the dead,
and the life of the world to come. Amen.

Taking in the View

We arrive finally at the concluding words of the Nicene Creed. Because we have been considering how the creed is a faithful map that brings us closer to God, let's look back and survey the ground we have covered thus far. We began with a forceful declaration that there is but one God, who is both immeasurably powerful and unfathomably close. This was an important beginning to claim, as it reinforces for our faith that God is both very real and very active in our lives. Next, we considered God the Son. This began with an exploration of his divinity and of how Jesus is of the same substance as God the Father.

In this, we saw how the Nicene Creed itself is critical for properly understanding our faith, as well-meaning Christians like Arius could arrive at heretical positions using Scripture alone.

Then, we considered Jesus's humanity, beginning with his earthly ministry from Christmas to Good Friday. Here, we traced how the Incarnation and the Crucifixion were not done flippantly, but rather "for us and for our salvation." In the next chapter, we explored Jesus's resurrection, ascension, and second coming with an eye toward how it was all done "in accordance with the Scriptures." This was important to note because it strengthens the continuity between the Old and New Testaments and the Nicene Creed.

Finally, in the last chapter, we moved to the Holy Spirit. By working through the initial Greek of the creed, we saw how the only way to worship the Trinity is together, together, together. The chapter ended by describing how the Spirit spoke to biblical characters and still speaks to us, leading us into greater understanding of truths that are contained within the treasuries of the Church like Scripture and the Nicene Creed.

This has been an important (and I hope enjoyable) journey so far. But the Nicene Creed does not exist unto itself as an abstract theological statement. As we've seen sprinkled throughout these chapters, the Nicene Creed was written as a tool for the Church to build up its faith. In its immediate context of AD 325, it shored up what was discerned to be the orthodox faith. And in our time, it still serves as a resource for the Church and for Christians to grow in discipleship. It is to this area, the establishment of the Church, that the creed turns in its final section.

On Your Marks

To begin this final section on the Church, the Nicene Creed makes a bold pronouncement: the Church is one, holy, catholic, and

One, Holy, Catholic, and Apostolic

apostolic. These characteristics have been called "the marks of the Church." We will consider each one in more detail in a moment, but even this first listing of the marks of the Church might have provoked a few questions. The foremost of these questions might be "Really?" That is, "Is the Church really one, holy, catholic, and apostolic?" Even putting aside the final two marks for the moment, which are not as commonly known, the matter isn't easier. Is the Church really one? Is it really holy?

As we discuss each of the marks below, we need to set some ground rules. There are a few ways to approach these characteristics, and some are less helpful than others. The first way is that of the Pessimists. Maybe you count yourself among this group (Pessimists don't call themselves "Pessimists"; they prefer the label "Realists"), or maybe you have some in your study group. Pessimists see this list and laugh. They dismiss the marks of the Church as idealistic hype that doesn't match reality. But as we'll see, the Pessimists must reckon with Scripture that seems to claim what the Nicene Creed says.

The next group is the Romantics. These aren't just optimists; they're Pollyannas who refuse to admit the Church might be anything but one, holy, catholic, and apostolic. Romantics wonder why we can't all just get along, and they believe that if we would just sit down and get to know one another, all our problems could be solved. But facts are what they are, and Christians aren't called to bury their heads in the sand, ignoring the problems facing Christ's Church.

A third group attempts to offer a middle ground. These are the Activists. These worker bees recognize that the Church has fallen short of what it has been called to be. The marks of the Church are, for them, marching orders. So wherever they see the Church is not one, holy, catholic and/or apostolic, they spring into action. I'm willing to bet you have a few of these in your church; thank God for go-getters like them! No church would last long without these folks filling our committees, getting to church before everyone else, and staying after everyone has left. Activists act as go-betweens and mediators to help make us one, they teach Sunday school classes to help make us holier, and on and on.

The problem with the Activists is that no amount of work seems to be enough. If the Church wasn't one, holy, catholic, and apostolic when it split between East and West in 1054 (see chapter 5), it only seems to have gone downhill since. No amount of bake sales or Bible studies is going to bring denominations back together or make us holy. The only results that Activists seem to achieve are turning people into Pessimists who have given up or Romantics who play pretend.

Instead, there's a fourth way. That is to be, as one author said, "an optimist of grace."[1] Optimists of Grace aren't optimistic because they believe the Church can work itself into being one, holy, catholic, and apostolic on its own. Instead, they are optimistic because God gives grace to the Church. Just as our individual salvation isn't a result of our works but rather our relying on God's saving grace, so it is with the Church. As another author puts it, "The church is holy because the Holy Trinity present in and to the church is holy."[2]

> **The marks of the Church are promises to live into, not benchmarks to measure up to.**

This isn't idle or frivolous hair-splitting. Optimists of Grace hold in balance the strengths of the other groups, all while holding even more tightly to God's grace. Optimists of Grace are like Pessimists because they admit that the Church falls short. They are like Romantics because they believe in a brighter future. And they are like Activists because they will work toward that goal. But unlike the

One, Holy, Catholic, and Apostolic

Activists, they work from a place of God's approval, not in search of it. As Paul writes, "For it is God who is at work in you, enabling you both to will and to work for his good pleasure" (Philippians 2:13). God works within the Church, and so the Church can work.[3] The marks of the Church are promises to live into, not benchmarks to measure up to.

With a proper understanding of the marks of the Church established, let's turn now to each mark in fuller detail.

One

This first mark of the Church is the plainest to understand. There is, as the creed suggests, "one" Church. Now, the Pessimists might chime in here and call attention to the fact that they can't drive from their home to their office without passing a dozen different kinds of churches. Plus, the more history-minded of the Pessimists might remind us that differences within Christianity have led to all sorts of conflicts, some deadly and some within our lifetime.

There is an old joke that illustrates this point. It goes like this: a man is marooned on a desert island for five years. Think Tom Hanks's character in *Cast Away*, except that he gets rescued while on the island. When the rescuers arrive, they notice that the man has constructed three huts out of branches and leaves.

The rescuers ask, "You've been all alone here. Why did you build three buildings?" The man responds, "Well, that first one is my house. The second is my church. And the third is the church I *used* to go to!"

This joke underscores a harsh reality: there really are a multitude of denominations and expressions of the Church. So, can the Church really be one? Let's see what Scripture has to say.

Several times in the New Testament, biblical authors speak of the "Church." This is the word translated from the Greek word *ekklesia*, which means "assembly" or, literally, "those called out." That is, Christians are those who are "called out" from the world and into fellowship together with God. In that sense, there is just one Church. God has called all of us out together; there have not been separate callings for Catholics, for Methodists, for Baptists, and so forth.

Another way that Paul speaks of the Church is to refer to it as the "body of Christ." Paul writes to the Corinthians, "For just as the body is one and has many members, and all the members of the body, though many, are one body, so it is with Christ. For in the Spirit we were all baptized into one body" (1 Corinthians 12:12-13). It's this line of thought that leads Paul ask sarcastically in the opening of that letter, "Has Christ been divided?" (1 Corinthians 1:13). Similar to our own denominational squabbles today, the Corinthians were divided and arguing with one another. Paul's point, then, about the Church being the body of Christ is that it can't be divided. Christ's body was broken once on the cross, but it was raised victoriously on the third day. If the full force of the world's sin could not keep Christ's body broken, then I seriously doubt that any number of denominations can.

What to do with all these denominations, then? We lean into that reality; we don't run from it. Maybe you are reading this right now in a small group setting with people of other denominations. Or maybe you have friends in other denominations. Praise God for that! The beauty and the purpose of the Nicene Creed is to provide a common bedrock for our faith.

Speaking of everyone who hears the Word of God, Jesus prayed to the Father that "they may all be one. As you, Father, are in me and I am in you, may they also be in us" (John 17:21). We believe that we have been called out as a Church not on our own but by God. Only the one who called us out in the first place can make us one. So let that be our prayer.

Holy

The next mark of the Church is that it is holy. Here, again, we run into immediate tension. I can't speak for every church and every congregation, but I am willing to bet that there are some decidedly unholy things in your church. There are the usual suspects: gossip, cliques, judginess, and caring more for ourselves than others. But even the Romantics can't ignore some more glaringly unholy behavior. Abuse of all kinds—spiritual, sexual, and physical—has happened within churches. I know of too many churches that have had funds intended for ministry embezzled. The list goes on.

Holy means "different or set apart by and for God." And yet, all too often, the Church doesn't look all that different from the world around us. Instead of looking like God, we look like the world. But we won't let the Pessimists take too much ground. Because, just like the Church's oneness, its holiness is not a result of its own merits. To restate the quote from above: "The church is holy because the Holy Trinity present in and to the church is holy." God has set the Church apart; it is holy by virtue of that gracious action.

This is supported by Scripture as well. Several times throughout the Old and New Testaments, God commands God's people to "be holy" (Leviticus 11:44-45; 19:2; 20:6; 1 Peter 1:15-16; relatedly, see Matthew 5:48). This has caused no small amount of heartburn in believers over the millennia. "Be holy? That's impossible!" we rightly cry. But as Jesus says, "For mortals it is impossible, but for God all things are possible" (Matthew 19:26). This is one area where my Methodist denominational heritage finds its strength. John Wesley, the founder of Methodism, saw commands like these as undergirded by promises. "Every command" in Scripture, said Wesley, "is only a covered promise."[4] The command to be holy is also a promise from the God who commanded it, because God is the only one who can make us holy. What God desires, God delivers. And this same command and promise that applies to Christians individually certainly applies to the gathered body of Christ, the Church.

Catholic

After the first two marks of the Church, which are common enough, the final two need defining. The Church, according to the Nicene Creed, is also "catholic." This term causes enough discomfort in some Protestant denominations that, in their printing of the Nicene and Apostles' creeds, the word *catholic* has an asterisk after it, with a helpful footnote explaining that catholic can also mean "universal."

But universal doesn't quite capture what the early Church meant by catholic. Catholic comes from the Greek expression *katholikos*. One of the meanings of *katholikos* is "universal," but the expression itself literally means "according to the whole." What the Council of Nicaea sought to capture by calling the Church "catholic" is that it is indeed the universal, or worldwide, community of believers. Because the Church is catholic, any Christian anywhere is part of the Church everywhere.

The meaning of catholic as "according to the whole" is also how we can speak not only of the universal Church (with a capital *C*) but also of individual churches (lowercase *c*). Paul can rightly begin his first letter to the Corinthians by saying, "To the church of God that is in Corinth" (1 Corinthians 1:2). He tells the church in Rome that he is commending "our sister Phoebe, a deacon of the church at Cenchreae" (Romans 16:1), to them. And he ends that letter by saying that "all the churches of Christ greet you" (Romans 16:16).

"All the churches"? But isn't the Church "one"? Yes, the Church is one, and we can speak of multiple churches within the Church precisely because the Church is also catholic. Each expression of the

Church, from the 1.3-billion-member Roman Catholic Church down to the smallest house church, is "according to the whole." They are all churches within the Church.

> **The Church being catholic also means that every Christian can find themselves a home within each branch of the Christian family.**

The Church being catholic also means that every Christian can find themselves a home within each branch of the Christian family. Just like a giant family reunion, there may be certain branches of that family that you feel closer to, more affinity with, and more comfortable in. But we're all family, connected by our catholicity and bounded by the Nicene Creed. On this point, consider a clergy colleague of mine. Bob was a Southern Baptist preacher in a city I served in a few years ago who decided that he wanted to switch denominations. So he became a deacon in the Eastern Orthodox Church! Looking at the Christian family tree, there are few branches farther apart than his old and new denominations. And while I am sure that much of his work changed in style, little changed in substance. Both churches, like all churches in the Church, hold to the faith expressed in the Nicene Creed and in Scripture.

Apostolic

The final mark of the Church is that it is "apostolic." The root of this word, as you may have guessed, is "apostle." As a specific term, this applies to the Twelve who were commissioned with establishing the Church in Acts,[5] as well as those others who were their contemporaries, including Paul. But the term "apostle" itself comes from the Greek verb *apostello*, which means "to send." In that sense, apostles are those who are sent on a mission and with a message.

There are a few ways that the Church has understood itself as apostolic. Some denominations, especially the Roman Catholic Church, understand being apostolic as meaning to be standing in an unbroken chain of leadership that reaches back to the original apostles. This is called "apostolic succession." Because leaders (such as bishops) in those denominations can only be consecrated in the presence of other leaders, a chain is formed linking even twenty-first-century bishops to the first generation of apostles. There are some incredibly beautiful and awe-inspiring charts depicting these chains of succession in various denominations. To make them fit on one page, the font for the names has to be very small; and because the Church is apostolic, the font will only continue to get smaller as more names are added!

I have something similar in my possession. In my own corner of the Christian world, the United Methodists of Oklahoma, every newly ordained pastor receives a chart like this in addition to their ordination certificate. Mine says that I was ordained by Bishop James Gregg Nunn. Bishop Nunn was himself ordained by Bishop Louis Wesley Schowengerdt, and on and on, until we get to John Wesley, the founder of Methodism. If we wanted, we could continue the chart, tracing Wesley's own ordination in the Church of England back to the first bishop in that denomination when it separated from the Roman Catholic Church. We might quibble about the zigs and zags in that chain, but in the Holy Spirit's power, the chain is unbroken.

Another way the Church has understood itself as apostolic is that its teachings trace back to the original apostles. The Church got its start after Pentecost by devoting itself "to the apostles' teaching and fellowship" (Acts 2:42), and it has continued doing so. Jude, in his short letter, exhorted his readers "to contend for the faith that was once and for all handed on to the saints" (Jude 3). The Church believes that these apostles, who were firsthand witnesses of Jesus and were the first recipients of the Holy Spirit at Pentecost, communicated the faith that we hold today.

It is no accident that the Council of Nicaea, meeting three hundred years after the apostles began their ministry, stressed that their church was still apostolic. What they were deciding and decreeing was not new; it came directly from the apostles' own teaching, as communicated in Scripture and handed down in church tradition.

It is for this reason that the most successful renewal movements in the Church's history began as attempts to return to the apostles' original teaching. Protestant Reformers, such as Martin Luther, followed the mantra *ad fontes*, or "to the sources." John Wesley, in his quest to revive the spirituality in his native Church of England, sought the "primitive Christianity" established in the period from the apostles to the Council of Nicaea. Even now, renewal movements in the Roman Catholic Church are drawing Catholics back to the earliest spiritual experiences and practices of the Church.

In every age and every expression of the Church, the Church balances these two approaches to its apostolicity. On the one hand, it delights in the development of its unbroken chain reaching back to the apostles. And on the other hand, it also knows that it can return to the original teaching and practice of the apostles. Like a beautiful cathedral, new wings and additions can be built on the strong foundation at the same time that older, original elements are being restored.

What the Church Is All About

We've just spent several paragraphs detailing what it means for the Church to be one, holy, catholic, and apostolic. It's easy, in deep discussions like those, to miss what is really at stake. At stake in discussing the marks of the Church is what the Church really is. There is a reason that the Council of Nicaea devoted such specific attention in their creed to the Church. The Church is the body of Christ, with a God-given mission in the world.

Consider a snapshot of what has gone on in my own local church in just the past week: Our Prayer Team has been in prayer for a toddler in our church who had to undergo heart surgery. In addition to prayer, folks are also cooking meals for the family, and one avid quilter is making a blanket to cover the child as a physical reminder of her church's love as she recovers. One of our ministry teams brought free pizza to a city park to feed kids in our community, and another brought a mason jar full of quarters to the local laundromat to pay for people's laundry. Finally, a new small group just formed from some of our new families of young adults. Led by a couple slightly older than them, this group is an answer to the question that had been raised recently by these young families: "Where can I belong?"

God's answer to that question is, emphatically, the Church. The Church is the place where insiders and outsiders alike are prayed over and provided for. One of the earliest images of the Church from around the time of the Council of Nicaea is of an ark. Just as Noah's ark provided refuge and deliverance for Noah, his family, and God's creation in Genesis 6–8, so the Church is God's vehicle for salvation in the world.

The Church, then, has a mission. As the "ark of salvation," the Church is meant to brave the world's tempestuous seas and offer rescue and relief, salvation and mercy, comfort and hope. Hence, Jesus could call his first disciples away from being fisherman to fishers of people (Matthew 4:19). Every Christian, by virtue of being aboard God's new ark, is a fisher of people. With Jesus as our captain and the Spirit as the wind in our sails, we embark on a mission.

This is why the marks of the Church are important. We aren't one, holy, catholic, and apostolic simply because those things are fun or important in their own right. Rather, they are mission-driven. The

Church is one because a ship rent in two won't stay afloat long. The Church is holy because it is set apart and distinct from the waters around it. The Church is catholic because a ship is made of different parts that function as a whole. And the Church is apostolic because its crew and officers have been trained by previous crews and officers, reaching all the way back to Jesus's original deckhands, the twelve disciples.

With a mission like this, who wouldn't want to be part of this ark of salvation, the Church! It's worth remembering this image the next time we feel bored or complacent in our churches. If boredom or complacency ever set in, it is likely an urging of the Spirit to set out for new, uncharted waters!

One Baptism

After detailing the marks of the Church, the creed asserts that "we acknowledge one baptism for the forgiveness of sins." This, as should be expected by now, comes directly from Scripture. Writing to the Ephesians, Paul stressed the unity of the Church. "There is one body and one Spirit, just as you were called to the one hope of your calling, one Lord, one faith, one baptism, one God and Father of all, who is above all and through all and in all" (Ephesians 4:4-6). This profound sentence not only reinforces the fact that the Church is one ("one body") and the truth of the Trinity (mentioning each member, "Spirit," "Lord," and "Father"), but it also says that there is "one baptism."

That is, in line with the Church's oneness and catholicity discussed above, there is just one entrance into the Church. Everyone gets in the same way: baptism. This baptism was inaugurated by John the Baptist, who proclaimed "a baptism of repentance for the forgiveness of sins" (Luke 3:3). In baptism, we die to our old lives of sin and are raised with Christ to new life. This rising is effective because it is done by God, hence only "one baptism" is required. As Jesus said, "One who has bathed does not need to wash...but is entirely clean" (John 13:10).

One note on this one baptism: the Church does require that baptism be done in the trinitarian format captured in the Nicene Creed. As Jesus commanded, we are to "make disciples of all nations, baptizing them in the name of the Father and of the Son and of the Holy Spirit" (Matthew 28:19). Baptisms that are done according to formulas other than the triune God are not considered valid. An illustration from the Book of Acts is helpful here. In Acts 18, we are introduced to Apollos, a well-meaning but misinformed preacher in Ephesus. He baptizes converts, but he doesn't know about the Holy Spirit. So when Paul comes through Ephesus in Acts 19, he meets these disciples of Apollos. When Paul asks them, "Did you receive the Holy Spirit when you became believers?" they reply, "No, we have not even heard that there is a Holy Spirit" (Acts 19:2). So Paul baptizes them, this time in the name of Jesus and the Holy Spirit. For this reason, people coming from faiths that do not confess faith in the triune God are baptized when they join a Christian church, even if their former faith practiced baptism of some kind. This is not rebaptism, because that first baptism was not a valid, trinitarian baptism.

The Resurrection and the Life

The Nicene Creed closes with a statement of our ultimate hope. "We look for the resurrection of the dead, and the life of the world to come." This is an expansion of one of the most comforting declarations from Jesus in John's Gospel. Right before he raises his friend Lazarus from the dead, Jesus speaks to Lazarus's sisters, Martha and Mary. He says to them, "I am the resurrection and the life. Those who believe in me, even though they die, will live, and everyone who lives and believes in me will never die" (John 11:25-26). Through Jesus's victorious resurrection, we are offered resurrection as well.

> **Through Jesus's victorious resurrection, we are offered resurrection as well.**

Speaking of the resurrection of the dead, Paul writes, "For this perishable body must put on imperishability, and this mortal body must put on immortality" (1 Corinthians 15:53). I have recited that verse at countless graveside services for church members, speaking to family and friends grieving the loss of a loved one. Those family members are in mourning, and God absolutely comforts those who mourn (see Matthew 5:4), but they are also hopeful as well. They are hopeful because this is the ultimate assurance of our faith, and the Council of Nicaea was cognizant to include this.

The phrasing of the second half of this sentence is important to unpack. We as Christians look for "the life of the world to come." The Greek word translated as "world" can also be translated as "age," as in a span of time. Most of the times it is used in the Bible, it refers either to our present reality or the future age of God's redeemed creation. It is this second reference in which the Nicene Creed refers to "the world to come."

The connection between resurrection and life in this final sentence of the creed is not accidental. Too much of religion these days treats eternity as an escape from life on earth. In that view, when our bodies die, our eternal souls rise up to heaven, where they remain forever with God. But that view, of an eternal soul but not body, is more Greek philosophy than biblical truth. To reiterate what Paul said in 1 Corinthians 15, our bodies are raised imperishable and immortal, not just our souls. Our life in "the world to come" will be embodied, just as Christ rose bodily.

This is the picture painted in the final two chapters of the Bible, Revelation 21–22. In those verses, John does not see souls floating up to a heavenly city in the clouds. Instead, he sees a "new earth" and a "new Jerusalem," where people live and where God lives with them. In the end, God's creation is not abandoned; it is redeemed.

Amen

The final word of the Nicene Creed is a familiar one. It is spoken most commonly at the end of a prayer, but many Christians aren't sure why that is. The word *amen* is a Hebrew word that made its way into the Greek New Testament because of its prevalence in the Jewish world of Jesus's and the apostles' day. There are a few different ways that different people have rendered the original meaning of *amen*, but a common translation is "let it be so."

That is, when someone finishes a prayer to God, extolling God's greatness or petitioning for something, those gathered around add their assent to what has been said. "Amen. Let it be so." Or it's why, when a preacher really hits their stride in a sermon and makes what they consider to be a good point, they ask, "Can I get an amen?" If the congregation is on board with things like this, an enterprising congregant will shout "Amen!" Let it be so.

And that is why, as the bedrock of our faith has just been laid out and recited in the Nicene Creed, it is only too appropriate to end with this word. The triune God has been named, the Son and the Spirit have been glorified in their proper place with the Father, our salvation has been announced, and the task of the Church has been established. Amen. Let it be so.

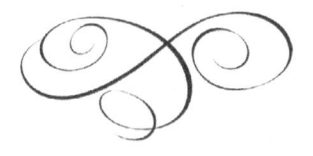

CONCLUSION
The Necessity of Nicaea Today

The Creed That Almost Wasn't

As we lookback with seventeen hundred years of hindsight, it can seem like the Council of Nicaea was the pinnacle of the Church's efforts to cement its core beliefs. As we've seen from the previous six chapters, everything that the authors of the Nicene Creed decreed could be traced back to Scripture and to following faithfully the Holy Spirit's guidance. While concepts not mentioned in Scripture, like the Trinity and *homoousios*, were developed at Nicaea, they were developed from Scripture. From this perspective, the Nicene Creed can seem inevitable, as if its words and doctrines were immediately destined to become the bedrock of Christian belief.

Nothing could be further than the truth.

Instead, the Nicene Creed was almost jettisoned entirely. From the council's adjournment in 325 until 360, most of its decisions were reversed or abandoned. The key term of the Nicene Creed, *homoousios*, was outright banned at one point.[1] This term, which was

Conclusion

discussed at length in chapter 2, indicates that God the Son is of the "same substance" (Greek: *homoousios*) as God the Father. This was the controversy that had led to the council's formation in the first place. And yet, despite the resounding victory of *homoousios* at the council, it was almost blotted from the Church's memory in thirty-five short years.

Its fortunes reversed yet again, however. By 381 and the convening of a new council in the city of Constantinople (mentioned in the introduction of this book), the Nicene Creed came roaring back to life. At Constantinople, the doctrines contained in the Nicene Creed were reinforced, enshrining Nicaea as the bedrock of Christian faith.

What was responsible for this seesaw? What led to Nicaea's near-abandonment in the decades after it, and what caused its resurgence fifty years later? The answer is both extraordinary and illustrative for us. If we want to have a faith made alive by the living truths of the Nicene Creed, we need to say a final word about how to make them take root within our souls, as they eventually did seventeen centuries ago.

The Councils after the Council

In the churches I've served, we have a tongue-in-cheek expression. You might use it in your church, too: "the meeting after the meeting." In my own Methodist tradition, we are no strangers to meetings. Our name came from an insult leveled at the first Methodists; they were too "methodical" about everything. That includes our penchant for committees, groups, and meetings. My church even has a committee responsible for putting people on committees!

Some of the meetings for these committees are life-giving and inspiring. Others are soul-sucking. All of them, though, usually have a "meeting after the meeting." At their most positive, these after-meetings continue the work of the primary meeting. As we walk to our cars, we are still excited about what we discussed, so we build onto and develop the plans we had made. I love these kinds of after-meetings. Other after-meetings are needed to clarify what the meeting had decided. Maybe a motion was made in the meeting that didn't explain clearly enough who was supposed to do what. Thus, this after-meeting is needed to clarify and enact what the meeting had intended.

The worst kind of after-meetings, however, are more nefarious. In these, certain people are excluded. Maybe it's the pastor; maybe it's the chair of the committee; maybe it's both! In any event, this after-meeting is called by disgruntled members of the committee who meet to discuss how they can undermine, overturn, or abandon what the meeting had decided. Maybe you've been the victim of an after-meeting like this. Or maybe you've been part of one!

The reaction to the Council of Nicaea had parts of all of these after-meetings. Some people left Nicaea excited about the council's decisions, and they wrote letters about how wonderful it was. Others wanted to clarify what the Nicene Creed said. They wrote treatises and books explaining the doctrines that Nicaea had decided. (This book stands in that proud tradition.)

Others, though, began to fight against Nicaea almost immediately. This included working to rehabilitate the image and status of Arius, whose heresy had been specifically condemned with the adoption of *homoousios*. It included cozying up to the emperor, using political power to chip away at the council's decisions. And it included calling new councils until the preferred outcome was achieved.

A Hero Emerges

Sitting in the Council of Nicaea was a minor participant who would grow to be the fiercest defender of the council. Athanasius was

Conclusion

a young priest living in the city of Alexandria when he attended the council as the personal secretary to his bishop, Alexander. We met Alexander in chapter 2 as one of the two primary combatants in the run-up to Nicaea; his debates with Arius over the relationship of God the Son to God the Father caused the Council of Nicaea in the first place.

What young Athanasius witnessed at the council must have made a lasting impression. After the council, he committed himself to the Nicene Creed as the truest summary of the faith, and he never looked back. Just a few months after returning from the council, Alexander died and Athanasius was named his successor. Athanasius worked tirelessly to defend the Nicene Creed, explain it, and ensure its survival. This did not go over well in the "after-meetings" discussed above. Over his years as bishop of Alexandria, Athanasius was exiled no fewer than five times, sometimes being forced to hide out in the Egyptian desert among the monks.

As the bishop of a city important to both the Roman Empire and the Church, Athanasius's life would have been much easier if he had hitched his wagon to the anti-Nicaea camp that was gaining power. He could have enjoyed imperial favor, the friendship of important leaders, and a controversy-free career. It would have been quite the feather in the cap of the anti-Nicaea forces if they had successfully flipped Athanasius from Nicaea-defender to Nicaea-detractor. Greater leaders have compromised for less.

But Athanasius is called "St. Athanasius the Great" for a reason. He gave no ground in compromising the truth of the faith that he saw contained in the Nicene Creed. It was Athanasius who "kept the name of Nicaea and the text of its creed alive, almost single-handedly at certain points."[2] But he was not inflexible. He would bend, but he would not break. Without abandoning the truth of the Nicene Creed, he worked with its detractors to convince them of its truth. He gained audiences with leaders inside and outside the Church, including the emperor himself, to plead his case, tailoring his arguments to his audience. And most effectively, he emboldened the next generation of church leaders to take up Nicaea's mantle.[3]

The Next Generation

Athanasius died in 373, a decade before Nicaea's ultimate victory. He died, then, not having seen his life's work accomplished. That task was left to the next generation of church leaders, especially Basil of Caesarea, whom we met in chapter 5, and his brother Gregory of Nazianzus. These men picked up where Athanasius had left off, carrying the Nicene Creed across the finish line.

In a relay race, each part of the race is important. The speed of each of the runners obviously has an effect on who reaches the finish line first. But just as important, if not more so, is the handoff between runners. The area where this occurs is called "the changeover zone." So much can go wrong in this zone. The runners might fumble the baton pass. The first runner might slow too much to ensure a smooth handoff that ultimately robs the team of precious seconds. Similarly, the second runner might not speed up enough before receiving the baton, so their leg begins slower than it should.

Passing the baton of Nicaea's defense was similar. Athanasius had to be faithful to the end, never slowing down in his championing of the Nicene Creed. Basil and Gregory had to be effective in their own right, gaining speed to match Athanasius's impact. And finally, Athanasius had to ensure that the actual handoff was successful. Nicaea could only be championed by people who adhered to the Nicene Creed.

All three of these things happened in the 360s and 370s. Athanasius, again, never wavered. He continued to write in defense

Conclusion

of the Nicene Creed until shortly before his death. Basil and Gregory, for their parts, became even more effective than Athanasius had been. In terms of rhetoric and persuasion, they were unmatched. Finally, the Nicene Creed was secured because this next generation had been carefully and deliberately brought up to believe in the truths of the creed.

> **The Nicene Creed was secured because this next generation had been carefully and deliberately brought up to believe in the truths of the creed.**

This all came to a victorious conclusion in 381 at the Council of Constantinople when the Nicene Creed was enshrined for good. There was no "meeting after the meeting" this time. This council provided an expanded version of the Nicene Creed, promulgated extra material to explain the creed, and decisively silenced critics. At the end of the day, the decisions at Constantinople "resonated with so many bishops, theologians, and church people in general at the time that lasting consensus was achieved."[4] Like in a relay race, Athanasius himself never crossed the finish line. But his faithfulness and perseverance, guided by the Holy Spirit, ensured the ultimate victory.

Transforming You

As I said in the introduction to this book, my church recites a creed every time we gather for worship. Most Sundays, we use the well-known Apostles' Creed, but often we will recite the Nicene Creed. On special occasions, like Trinity Sunday, we even break out the Athanasian Creed! (If you're unfamiliar with this creed attributed to Athanasius, look it up sometime; it's a doozy!) We recite these creeds toward the end of worship, in our time of response after

Conclusion

hearing the Word of God read and preached. Along with our time of offering, celebrating Holy Communion, and performing baptisms or receiving new members when applicable, reciting the creed is the way we respond as a church family in worship. And over the past couple years, something incredible has happened.

A few years ago, we moved the time of our children's Sunday school. Instead of having it occur during worship, like it used to be, it was moved to before worship. So now, children and youth sit in the sanctuary with their families for the entire worship service. You can imagine the adjustment this required; we had much more fidgeting, whispering, and shushing than we used to! But we never once thought about going back. Because now our children hear the Lord's Prayer, the creeds, and the Communion liturgy, among other things.

Here's the best part: our teenagers have developed a fun game during worship. When I get up to lead the creed, I direct the congregation to open their hymnals or look at the Sanctuary screen to find the words. But not our teenagers! They make unbroken eye contact with me the entire time. They do this not only to show me that they have it memorized; I think they also do it to make sure I do, too!

These young people have figured out the life-giving power of the Nicene Creed. They've figured out that the words of the creed aren't just lifeless phrases to repeat like robots. The words of the creed are empowering, exciting, and even challenging! They have a passion for worship and for our faith that gives me hope for the Church's future.

I'm not naive, though. I know that, statistically, some of the teenagers in my church right now won't stay connected to their faith into their college and young adult years. And yet, I have hope. Because they've memorized the Nicene Creed. So no matter what happens in their life, no matter how long they may live in the "far country" with the prodigal son (Luke 15:13 KJV), the Spirit-inspired words of the

Conclusion

creed will be with them. In moments of crisis, they might remember "*We believe in one God, the Father, the Almighty.*" When they feel alone, they might remember the words "*For us and for our salvation he came down from heaven.*" When they wonder what their purpose in life is, perhaps these words will come to them: "*We believe in the Holy Spirit, the Lord, the giver of life.*" And like a trustworthy map, the creed will lead them back to God.

This is the power of the Nicene Creed. This is why Christians have recited and clung to it for seventeen hundred years. And it is why Christians will still be reciting it seventeen hundred years from now. The words of the creed have an ability to burrow into our hearts and into the deepest reaches of our minds. They connect us to the living core of our faith. When combined with other things like Scripture reading, corporate worship, and prayer, the Nicene Creed breathes a life into your faith that makes it exciting and joy-filled. What's more, the Nicene Creed also holds the potential to reinvigorate your church.

Transforming Your Church

You may have read through this book in a class at your local church. If that's the case, I also suspect that you have a hint as to how the Nicene Creed can strengthen your church. Over these chapters, your group has discussed these core elements of our faith. You've had discussions, questions, and maybe even a few arguments! But through it all, you have stuck together. And most important, you have been active participants in your faith.

The Nicene Creed invites participation and ownership. There is a reason that the pronouns at the beginning of each section of the creed are "we" and not "I" or, worse, "you." The creed is not something to be said only by yourself or on your own. And it's also not something that your pastor gets up and declares on your behalf: "*You believe in*

Conclusion

one God..." Instead, you declare it next to the other people in your church family: the same people you serve alongside, the same people you love as an adopted family, and, sometimes, the same people who frustrate you to no end!

If your church doesn't do this already, incorporating a creed into your worship service will strengthen your faith and fellowship immensely. It will, at the very least, remind your church family of the living core of your faith. If the sermon isn't that good one Sunday (I'll be honest, some of my sermons are flat-out duds), I can always rest assured knowing that our church proclaimed the gospel in the creed! And more than that, reciting the creed will increase participation on the part of the church family. The word *liturgy* literally means "the work of the people," so we should take every chance we can get to shift that work from the pastor and leaders back to the people. We're called to "exercise" our faith for a reason! Finally, as we saw above with the youth in my church, reciting the creed regularly in your church will plant seeds of faith that will burrow deeply. You might not see fruit immediately, but it will come.

And if your church does already regularly recite the creed in worship, great! If it has become a chore or a rote task to be checked off every week, now is the time to change that. All it takes is a few well-placed people in the pews to change the atmosphere in worship. Next Sunday, when you say the creed, say it with feeling! Maybe even say it more slowly, giving each word its full effect. (Remember the "together, together, together" in chapter 5?) Make it into a competition—see who in your family or small group can memorize the creed first. Prizes will be awarded in the form of a contagious, irresistible faith!

Give it a year, and I guarantee that reciting the creed in worship with passion and purpose will reinvigorate your church. It will make members of your church family more excited about worship, and it will make your church a more attractive place for newcomers. There

Conclusion

is something about a seventeen-hundred-year-old statement of faith that is appealing to people in our world. So much of the focus in society is on newness and novelty; people long for a connection to something that lasts and will outlast them. Reciting the creed will give them that.

> **There is something about a seventeen-hundred-year-old statement of faith that is appealing to people in our world.**

Finally, realizing that each of us has been called out into Christ's holy Church together, reinvigorating the use of the creed in worship would help us recapture the passion and Spirit that inspired the Council of Nicaea seventeen centuries ago. We would be one, holy, catholic, and apostolic Church.

Amen. Let it be so.

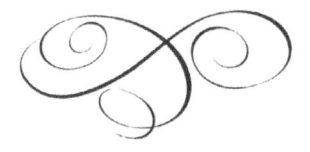

NOTES

Introduction

1. The figure of 318 bishops is debated by scholars. It is argued that 318 is symbolic, lining up with the number of Abraham's servants listed in Genesis 14:14. Modern analyses suggest a lower number, 250–300. See David M. Gwynn, "Reconstructing the Council of Nicaea," in *The Cambridge Companion to the Council of Nicaea*, ed. Young Richard Kim (Cambridge: Cambridge University Press, 2021), 92–96.
2. C. S. Lewis, *Mere Christianity* (New York: HarperCollins, 1980), 153–155.

Chapter 1: We Believe in One God

1. All biblical references are taken from the NRSV Updated Edition (NRSVue) unless otherwise noted.
2. A more precise term is *Christ Pantocrator*, with the Greek word *pantocrator* meaning "almighty."
3. Arnobius, "Praise for the Indescribable," in *Fount of Heaven: Prayers of the Early Church*, ed. Robert Elmder (Bellingham, WA: Lexham Press, 2022), 20.

Chapter 2: Of One Being with the Father

1. Rebecca Lyman, "Arius and Arianism," in Kim, *The Cambridge Companion to the Council of Nicaea* (Cambridge: Cambridge University Press, 2021), 51.
2. Romans 1:7; 1 Corinthians 1:3; 2 Corinthians 1:2; Galatians 1:3; Ephesians 1:2; Philippians 1:2; 2 Thessalonians 1:2; Philemon 3;

Notes

for similar introductions, see also Colossians 1:3; 1 Thessalonians 1:1; 1 Timothy 1:2; 2 Timothy 1:2.

3 "Article V – Of the Sufficiency of the Holy Scriptures for Salvation," *The Book of Discipline of The United Methodist Church* 2016 (Nashville: The United Methodist Publishing House, 2016), 66.

4 The theologian and Methodist pastor William Abraham coined the term "canonical theism" to describe this rich tradition.

Chapter 3: For Us and for Our Salvation

1 The word for "our" used here in the Creed is *hemeteran*, which appears only eight times in the New Testament. The regular form for "our," *hemon*, is used over four hundred times.

2 St. Athanasius, *On the Incarnation*, trans. John Behr (Yonkers, NY: St. Vladimir's Seminary Press, 2011), 59. Emphasis added.

3 W. H. Auden, *For the Time Being: A Christmas Oratio*, ed. Alan Jacobs (Princeton: Princeton University Press, 2013), 8.

4 C. S. Lewis, *Miracles* (San Francisco: HarperOne, 2015).

5 St. Athanasius, *On the Incarnation*, 89.

6 Henry H. Knight III helpfully expounds on this in *Anticipating Heaven Below* (Eugene, OR: Cascade Books, 2014), 40.

Chapter 4: In Accordance with the Scriptures

1 St. Basil the Great, *On the Holy Spirit*, trans. Stephen Hildebrand (Yonkers, NY: St. Vladimir's Seminary Press, 2011), 41n18.

2 J. R. R. Tolkien, *The Lord of the Rings* (New York: Houghton Mifflin Harcourt, 2021), 758.

3 Fleming Rutledge, "Loving the Dreadful Day of Judgment," in *Advent: The Once and Future Coming of Jesus Christ* (Grand Rapids, MI: William B. Eerdmans, 2018), 182.

4 N. T. Wright, *The Day the Revolution Began* (New York: HarperOne, 2016).

Chapter 5: With the Father and the Son

1 St. Basil, *On the Holy Spirit*, 9.22.

2 Stephen E. Broyles, "What Do We Mean by 'Godhead'?" *The Evangelical Quarterly* 50, no. 4 (1978): 223–229.

3 This is the same reason why the word *ghost* has an *h*. Five hundred years ago, all words that began with a hard *g* had an *h* after it. This was slowly removed from most words, but *ghost* was left alone because the King James Version spoke of the Holy Ghost, and to remove the *h* from *ghost* would be to change the Word of God.
4 Athanasian Creed, https://www.ccel.org/creeds/athanasian.creed.html.
5 Timothy I, "The Apology of Timothy the Patriarch Before the Caliph Mahdi," trans. Alphonse Mingana, *Bulletin of the John Rylands Library* 12, no. 1 (1928): 205.
6 Timothy I, "Apology of Timothy," 206.
7 Geoffrey D. Dunn, "Catholic Reception of the Council of Nicaea," in Kim, *The Cambridge Companion to The Council of Nicaea* (New York: Cambridge University Press, 2021), 353. Emphasis mine.
8 St. Basil, *On the Holy Spirit*, 18.45.
9 Paul L. Gavrilyuk, "The Council of Nicaea in the Orthodox Tradition," in Kim, *The Cambridge Companion to the Council of Nicaea*, 341. Emphasis mine.
10 Gavrilyuk, "Council of Nicaea," 341.
11 St. Basil, *On the Holy Spirit*, 23.54.

Chapter 6: One, Holy, Catholic, and Apostolic

1 Henry H. Knight III, *John Wesley: Optimist of Grace* (Eugene, OR: Cascade Books, 2018). Knight was speaking of John Wesley when he used this term. I find this term illustrative and instructive not only because Wesley is the progenitor of my theological tradition but also because Wesley embodied the approach advocated for in this chapter.
2 Jason Vickers, *Minding the Good Ground: A Theology for Church Renewal* (Waco: Baylor University Press, 2011), 37.
3 This sentiment is expressed by John Wesley in his sermon "On Working Out Your Own Salvation" with the words: "First, God works; therefore you *can* work. Secondly, God works, therefore you *must* work." John Wesley, "On Working Out Our Own Salvation: Sermon 85 – 1785," in *John Wesley's Sermons: An Anthology*, ed. Albert C. Outler and Richard P. Heitzenrater (Nashville: Abingdon Press, 1991), 490.

Notes

4 John Wesley, "Upon Our Lord's Sermon on the Mount, Discourse V: Sermon 25 – 1728," in Outler and Heitzenrater, *John Wesley's Sermons: An Anthology* (Nashville: Abingdon Press, 1991), 211.

5 This Twelve includes Matthias, who was chosen by the remaining eleven to replace Judas (see Acts 1:12-26).

Conclusion

1 Sara Parvis, "The Reception of Nicaea and *Homoousios* to 360," in Kim, *The Cambridge Companion to the Council of Nicaea*, 225.

2 Parvis, "Reception of Nicaea," 254.

3 Parvis, "Reception of Nicaea," 254.

4 Mark DelCogliano, "The Emergence of the Pro-Nicene Alliance," in Kim, *The Cambridge Companion to the Council of Nicaea*, 280.

Watch videos based on *We Believe: How the Nicene Creed Can Deepen Your Faith* with Michael Carpenter through Amplify Media.

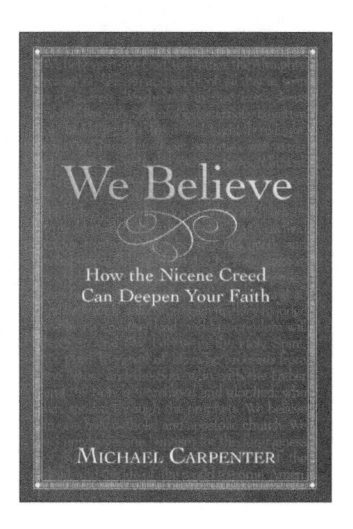

Amplify Media is a multimedia platform that delivers high-quality, searchable content with an emphasis on Wesleyan perspectives for churchwide, group, or individual use on any device at any time. In a world of sometimes overwhelming choices, Amplify gives church leaders and congregants media capabilities that are contemporary, relevant, effective and, most important, affordable and sustainable.

With *Amplify Media* church leaders can:

- Provide a reliable source of Christian content through a Wesleyan lens for teaching, training, and inspiration in a customizable library
- Deliver their own preaching and worship content in a way the congregation knows and appreciates
- Build the church's capacity to innovate with engaging content and accessible technology
- Equip the congregation to better understand the Bible and its application
- Deepen discipleship beyond the church walls

⋀ AMPLIFY. MEDIⴷ

Ask your group leader or pastor about Amplify Media and sign up today at www.AmplifyMedia.com.

Made in United States
Cleveland, OH
06 July 2025